THE SOCIAL MEDIA SURVIVAL GUIDE FOR POLITICAL CAMPAIGNS:

Everything You Need to Know to
Get Your Candidate Elected Using Social Media

Sherrie A. Madia, Ph.D.

Full Court Press

Full Court Press
A Division of Base Camp Communications, LLC
3 Woodstone Drive
Voorhees, NJ 08043

Find Us Online:
SocialMediaSurvivalGuideForPoliticalCampaigns.com

Library of Congress Cataloging-in-Publication Data
Madia, Sherrie Ann
The Social Media Survival Guide for Political Campaigns / by Sherrie Madia.

Summary: Best practices for implementing online tactics designed to activate the voter base and win elections.
  p. cm.

ISBN: 978-0-9826185-4-7

2011934543

Printed in the United States of America

10 9 8 7 6 5 4 3 2 1 First Edition

CONTENTS

ACKNOWLEDGMENTS

RESEARCHING FOR PROJECTS such as this is never the work of just one individual. My grateful thanks go to the talented individuals who helped to bring this book to fruition through their diligent efforts, including Adrienne Benson Scherger, Amanda Brandon, Jane Genova, Leann Harms, Jason Karpf, Kristie Lorette, Dan Manning, Lori Moore, Robert Moskowitz, Minnie Payne, Linda Rosencrance, Brooke Rothman and Kathy Shaidle. And thanks for the practitioners, politicos, and campaign offices all of whom were gracious enough to share their own accounts. I hope this book proves useful in the ever-evolving and always adrenalized landscape of the political campaign.

INTRODUCTION

HAVING SPENT MORE THAN two decades of my career as a practitioner and academic in the field of professional communications, the shift in focus to social media was simply a natural progression as technologies and users of technology continue to evolve. But unlike other movements within communications, social media provides such rapid iterations of content and distribution of content that it has become a direct reflection of an organization's and an individual's relevance. When brought to the political arena, it is now a requirement in any campaign.

In shaping the scope of *The Social Media Survival Guide* series several years ago, I began with two core areas of application: social media and business and social media and job search. With the success of *The Social Media Survival Guide: How to Grow Your Business Exponentially with Social Media*, and *The Online Job Search Survival Guide: How to Use Social Networking to Land a Job Now*, I was afforded many opportunities to hear from people from across industries and organizations—from small business owners to NGOs, to government officials, people looking to reinvent themselves and jump-start their careers, nonprofits looking to compete differently and more effectively in the marketplace, and others in between.

The invaluable conversations demonstrate that as users, as consumers and as strategists, we can make no assumptions when it comes to social media. Thus, two additional areas of application, and two additional books were added to the *Social Media Survival Guide* series: social media for nonprofits, and social media for political campaigns, each offering nuances particular to incorporating social media tactics into existing strategies for optimal effect.

Like everything else, people who are tasked with implementing social media want the one-hit, simple approach. Hence, the question, "What is 'the best' platform I should be using to reach my audience?" followed swiftly by, "Just tell me what I need to do so we can say we're 'on' social media." The answer, of course, is never so simple, and social media is not about standard-order anything. Sure, there are baseline elements your campaign should have, but the implementation and content generation should be anything but cookie-cutter. Social media is about an ongoing and meaningful conversation toward a longer, deeper relationship. And it is never an exercise in "set it and forget it."

To offer a simple analogy, would you preset your conversations with a best friend from now through the next six months? Would you ask this friend an important question and then simply walk away before hearing the response? If the friend wanted Chinese food instead of Italian, would you go Italian anyway because that was your original plan?

Chances are you would be a bit more fluid, more iterative, and more apt to let each situation unfold in real time. And chances are you and your friend would repeat this process again and again, communicating regularly to keep one another up to date. Isn't that what friends do? This is the same approach you must take in garnering supporters to back your campaign. Treat them as friends in the sense that you must work to build the relationship and to keep it working productively. When we view social media through this lens, it isn't so new or foreign after all.

Regardless of whether you are running a campaign or an

organization with a cause that needs backing, you must begin with the basics of knowing your objective, your audience, and your resources, and then shaping a strategy and tactics designed to support this.

Each election brings with it a new approach to campaigning. Professionals leading campaign efforts must be cognizant that the landscape has changed when it comes to research, building a base of support, engagement, endorsement, raising funds, and getting voters out to the polls. Campaign directors who are able to successfully harness social media as part of their overall strategy will find opportunities to drive their candidates to victories like never before.

Political campaigns are built upon a candidate's ability to appear more active than reactive, to drive core, consistent messages to the right groups of potential supporters at the right time, and to create ongoing engagement opportunities for constituents. Those who bypass the strategies that social media presents will be missing the chance to be iterative and creative, and to make often tight resources work harder and more effectively.

What used to take weeks, months or the length of a campaign to figure out, can now be determined in real time, and with deeper involvement from would-be supporters—and open detractors. *The Social Media Survival Guide for Political Campaigns* will arm campaign managers, directors, and volunteer committees with simple ways to start building social media tactics into more traditional campaigns for a smarter way to win elections.

But it is not enough merely to offer strategies for success. Hence, this text includes snapshots of campaigns and governments that have implemented these strategies. In addition to U.S. examples, several global examples have been showcased to offer some perspective into the global landscape, which is an important consideration in all that we do pertaining to government, at all levels and across the globe.

Like a campaign organizer, the American public must approach any upcoming election knowing that massive efforts are underway to sway its opinions.

Social media takes these efforts to a new level—and citizens must pay close attention.

The 2008 presidential election demonstrated the power of interactive, online engagement in producing grassroots efforts designed to win elections. This presidential election also showed that the public must be diligent in determining its choice for elected office by continuing to assess the message along with the medium.

Today's elections at the local, state, and federal levels are simply too important to the future of the country amidst ongoing economic, social, and political upheaval. Each and every voter is in a position to engender significant change, and each voter must be presented with a personal, engaging reason to do so.

Knowing how social media can and will be used in future elections—and how voters might harness these powers to help the cause or candidate they support—is an opportunity to position voters as the active, dynamic voices they were meant to be within any vote.

The Social Media Survival Guide for Political Campaigns offers insights to voters that will help them to understand how they are being courted by political interests, as well as how they can help to rally support at the community level.

On so many fronts, social media helps to solve the existing enigmas we have been grappling with in political and cause-based campaigns. That includes how to get target groups of citizens engaged or reengaged, and how to generate an event, a message, or an element of engagement that will elicit opt-in participation; and more importantly, how to engage target groups—members, volunteers, elected officials, board members, corporate interests, clubs, associations, donors—in a manner that generates organic, peer-to-peer connection to give under-resourced campaigns more feet on the street on behalf of their cause or position.

Despite the insistence from some pundits that lack of campaign funds alone is not a disqualifier (and John McCain proved this out in the 2008 presidential elections), still, a well-funded campaign offers flexibility and the ability of a campaign to be agile in the voting arena. Thus, fundraising can never be discounted as a nice to have.

As a powerful network of distribution channels, social media platforms have the ability to address the most pressing needs of any campaign taking a strategic and thoughtful approach to what these online tools can do—and keeping in mind that everything we do in the online space is about a real-world effect.

The sophistication of political campaigns and their constituencies can be dramatically diverse within local, state and even national elections. Those campaigns that are able to become first-adopters of the latest trends in communications technologies—will afford themselves more than campaign contributions alone can provide. That is, today's campaign organizers have a unique opportunity to capitalize on the many new touch points of engagement that will become the hallmarks of effective campaigning—opportunities to give a strong voice to citizens and groups who have otherwise gone unnoticed, a chance to cast a wider net in targeted populations to garner volunteer support, and an opportunity to shape and fine tune the campaign message as the campaign unfolds based on real-time knowledge learned via comments and other user-generated content.

Social media brings to the political campaign a new raison d'etre in terms of constituent relations. Social media, which, simply defined, is a new set of engagement strategies, enables campaigns to work from a level playing field, regardless of budget. While campaign directors may think that social media means *more* work, what it really means is *different* and often more effective work in that it is based on the principles of time-shifted, 24/7, as-they-like-it content, with a dose of user-generated fare to sustain the need for ongoing dialogue. It is the perfect storm for meeting the longest-standing need of the political campaign: reaching out to as many potential supporters as possible.

The Obama campaign proved that strategic use of social media has the ability to propel a political campaign to a successful outcome in ways that longtime politicians and campaign directors had never before experienced—everything from text messages from campaign headquarters, to Facebook fan pages from organizer groups—all tied to real, effective action.

With the ongoing adoption of social media by the mainstream, upcoming elections at the local, state, and federal level must arm themselves with a new set of tactics designed to capture voters' attention—or risk losing out on vital campaign contributions, not to mention growing and mobilizing a strong base of support.

The pages that follow provide the new toolkit for success—from pitfalls to avoid to practical baseline tactics—that every campaign communicator must understand in order to affect a winning election. Topics include why today's campaign manager must understand how social media channels can yield rapid support and propel a candidate's chances for victory; how to strategize a candidate's positioning and create a personal brand that showcases core issues and campaign messages; how to engage online support for tangible effects in the form of volunteer support, fundraising, the Online Townhall, voter turnout and more.

Social media tactics enable campaign organizers to not only

target their donor base more effectively, but also target additional pools of constituents that they may not have considered in a pre-Web 2.0 environment. Also discussed are strategic uses of social media designed to engage, cultivate, activate, and motivate citizens utilizing social media techniques. Tapping into social networks enables those responsible for reaching constituents and raising volunteer and fundraising support to optimize their efforts by adding value and delivering this value to supporters and potential supporters in a manner that is flexible and extensible as the campaign progresses.

If you are charged with overseeing anything from a local campaign fundraiser to a national, high-profile campaign—whether you are working from a shoestring budget or a surplus, this text will arm you with the tools you need to rally your base of support by creating additional touch points of engagement and bringing the life cycle of the voter full circle by optimizing opportunity within the interactive, digital space.

CHAPTER 1

Online Campaigning for
Real-World Effects

I N COFFEE SHOPS, BOARD ROOMS, local businesses and
global corporations, everyone is talking about social media.
Across industry, levels of education and awareness, or actual
usage, people are intrigued by social media, social networking, and
social marketing. Reactions to social media have been as diverse
as chalking it up to hype and a passing fad, to organizations and
individuals running at social media platforms at breakneck speed.
Somewhere between these two extremes is where your political
campaign should be.

Even several years back, it was okay to maintain a healthy
skepticism about social media—after all, with limited resources,
campaign organizers must be smart with how they spend their
financial and human resources. But in the brief span of history
that marks the era of social media, we have amassed sufficient data
to tell us that certain elements of social media—beginning with
the premise of deeper and more authentic engagement between
consumer and brand, client and provider, constituent and cause—
are here to stay.

State Representative Justin Amash (R-Michigan) understands this power of engagement. In June 2009, he began posting each of his votes in the Michigan House of Representatives along with an explanation of why he voted the way he did on a Facebook fan page he had created. The response was overwhelmingly positive, with constituents thanking Amash for cluing them in.

Amash's Facebook updates center on the most important social media consideration: value. He understands his audience and their needs, as reflected in this update from December 24, 2010 in which he writes:

Check out the new tool at http://michiganvotes.org/ that lets you see how often a state legislator voted against the majority of that person's party. Top 5: (1) Justin Amash, 471/1,314 (votes cast); (2) Tom McMillin, 326/1,313; (3) Bob Genetski, 269/1,256; (4) Dave Agema, 246/1,314; (5) Tory Rocca, 225/1,296.[1]

This Facebook fan page provides the perfect forum for offering authenticity, credibility, and the transparency that citizens are craving from their elected officials. And building this relationship with constituents early can create a distinct advantage for any candidate's upcoming campaign in that not only has a core of supporters gotten to know the candidate already, but potential supporters can ascertain the character of the candidate right away via the candidate's proven public record of honesty and sincerity with the voters. While this exercise can be time-consuming in that the point is not just to push information, but to respond to and engage in dialogue with constituents, it is a strategy well worth undertaking for any candidate considering a run down the road.

Information consumers have found that being given a voice and the ability to contribute to the story of a brand or a cause or an individual feels good—and it feels empowering. It is emotionally and psychologically satisfying to tell our stories, share our comments, offer our insights—and to actually be heard and responded to. We simply will not give up this newfound power any time soon.

And organizations have found that enabling consumers, clients, and constituents to help tell their stories also makes sense. Across the board, organizations have determined that the rewards of authentic, organic engagement delivered in a more intimate and targeted way far outweigh the risks, which can include negative comments, opinions, and concerns that content creators hadn't planned for.

Given the resulting combination of hype, rapid iterations of social networking platforms (e.g., Google+ launched in July 2011 and in just two weeks had 10 million users), and real value that these platforms provide, the social media space naturally presents a tempting new arena for political campaigns to explore in terms of targeting volunteers and supporters, generating funds, and creating overall impact that results in a winning election.

In discussing the transformative power of social media in a similar sector—non-profits— Dave Kerpen, CEO of the social media leveraging firm Likeable Media, notes, "Not only can tools such as Facebook and Twitter help raise funds and awareness for organizations, they can strengthen relationships between supporters and the cause, as well as among stakeholders."

Recent experience provides ample evidence that every campaign—from local, to state, to national—can benefit greatly from the additional points of engagement and the tools for turning uninformed citizens into ardent supporters and active voters.

What the 2010 Midterm Elections Told Us

A study by the Pew Research Center Internet and American Life Project[2] shows that social media became a standard campaign element in the 2010 midterm elections. This research showed that 22 percent of Americans used social media to research, learn more, and to better connect on a personal level with a candidate. Specifically, the study notes:

- 11 percent of online adults discovered on a social networking site who their friends voted for in the November elections
- 9 percent of online adults received candidate or campaign information on social networking sites or Twitter
- 8 percent of online adults posted political content on Twitter or a social networking site
- 7 percent of online adults friended a candidate or political group on a social networking site, or followed that candidate on Twitter
- 7 percent of online adults started or joined a political group on a social networking site
- 1 percent of online adults used Twitter to follow the election results as they were happening[3]

The story these figures tell is that those who are politically motivated will seek out information via social networks and will look to engage with friends on the issues as another source of information within their community.

Juan C. Torres, MD, Founder of the Latino American Tea Party (http://LatinoAmericanTeaParty.org/), understands this concept and has used it to rally support around key issues by keeping members informed. Through email messages to members and interested parties, Dr. Torres sends links to relevant news articles, petitions, commentary and more from top political sites, thereby offering convenience and relevance delivered by a credible source directed primarily to conservative-minded Latinos. With media outlet biases now a blatant part of the political landscape, the role of "trusted advisor" in the form of average citizens serving as third-party intermediaries for fellow citizens and voters will continue to take on a vital role in elections.

From a C-Span panel on social media and political campaigns[4], Mindy Finn, Republican new media strategist, noted that for Sean Duffy, now Congressman Duffy, representing the seventh district of Wisconsin, social media drove him from an unknown to a candidate who was able to oust a known commodity—longtime political figure David Obie, chairman of the appropriations committee. The latter decided to drop out of the race and retire.

In part this was because Duffy, a former MTV's *Real World* star, knew more than a year ago that he would run for office. Therefore, he began carrying a flipcam with him, documenting his campaign activities, and posting videos on YouTube. Because Duffy is also a lumberjack, his collection included a video of himself and his family going out to cut down a Christmas tree. He was personable, engaging, and authentic on video, which helped him to take on the well-known Obie.

New Jersey Governor Chris Christie Leverages Campaign Budget to Win in 2009

Gubernatorial candidate Chris Christie had a problem. In 2009, he was running against incumbent Governor of New Jersey Jon Corzine, who had a budget three times the size of his, and Christie was running in a state that had not seen a Republican governor in more than a decade. Christie's initial television ad spends were targeting people between the Philadelphia and New York markets, which meant that many of the voters viewing the ads could not even vote because they were out of state.

The Christie campaign turned to a more targeted and economical approach by mobilizing a group of online supports they had been building since the start of the campaign, and then targeting ads and repeat messaging to those who had clicked through to Christie's website.

In addition, the Christie campaign was the first in the U.S. to deploy Google video ads. Those ads were housed on YouTube (also great for added visibility) and then distributed via a click-to-play-video structure, thus saving the campaign countless dollars in broader, less targeted television commercials.

The campaign also used social media banners to engage new constituents by enabling them to click through right from the banner to follow Christie on a variety of social media channels.

These efforts proved to be key strategies in leveling the playing field between a campaign with big money and the Christie campaign. The online marketing efforts helped to combat some of the harshest attack ads in the nation, by enabling a rapid response mechanism, resulting in a Christie victory of 49 percent to Corzine's 45 percent.

CampaignGrid's new media campaign helps Chris Christie win NJ governor's race. http://www.campaigngrid.com/_blog/Case_Studies/post/CampaignGrid's_New_Media_Campaign_helps_Chris_Christie_win_NJ_Governor's_Race/ n.d. Web 4 November 2009.

Overall reported uses for social media by political campaigns include communicating with volunteers and staff, facilitating public awareness and education, finding new fundraisers, general networking, promoting positions on important issues, prospecting for campaign volunteers and donors, researching, and exchanging information with like-minded constituents.

Your Campaign Needs Social Media

While 2008 marked a coming-out party for social media as a means of tapping into the voter population in a new and more personal way, in the 2012 elections, social media will simply become a campaign necessity. While social media is varied and flexible enough to support a wide range of human activity, at present the most popular and promising uses among political campaigns include the following:

Fundraising

Two years into his first term, President Obama's campaign committee began circulating a 12-slide presentation on the 2012 incumbent's increased need for fundraising dollars from would-be supporters.[5]

Campaign hopefuls for any election must begin their fundraising efforts early and online.

To facilitate this, each campaign site should make it easy for website visitors to learn about the candidate, its mission, goals, objectives and positions on core issues. The site should also have a "Donate Now" button on every page that brings potential donors straight to a form that allows quick and easy gifting, preferably with an option to use a credit card or other online giving mechanisms such as PayPal.

Internal and External Communications

Social media is not a one-way communication: it is focused on the idea of the conversation, and as such, is well suited as a vehicle for sharing information and receiving feedback among the various stakeholders associated with a non-profit. Messages to campaign volunteers, staff, key media contacts, and others can be personalized through social media, which can be set up to facilitate both individual responses and more widespread sharing based on organizational and social media policies.

Listening Infrastructure

Social media also offers opportunities to simply listen. By helping stakeholders communicate with each other, as well as provide feedback, your campaign can develop a detailed map of the interests and preferences of people who connect with you, as well as any positive and negative impressions they may have formed. This is powerful, qualitative data to incorporate as you fine tune messages, develop new, programmatic initiatives, reach out to new audiences, and attract more support.

Message Building

In addition, social media permits key members of a political campaign to develop and build the various sets of messages to be communicated to the public, and to coordinate the dissemination of these messages by making sure every potential spokesperson and campaign envoy is on the same page—this becomes a vital communications consideration in the wake of media-savvy constituencies and voter communities.

So, for example, it is not unusual to see a candidate float some new messaging out within a post, an update, or an online townhall, thus gauging reaction and modifying the message as necessary before launching untested content within a costly television ad or direct-mail piece.

Community Building

Social media is also fundamental for building an online community, which can greatly increase the online footprint and thus, the visibility and credibility of any candidate. One caveat is that while building online communities can begin to feel like the universe, it is a mistake to become so enraptured with this work that the campaign neglects its traditional offline communities—particularly volunteers, donors, and other supporters who may not be as heavily involved online, but who are vital in helping to get a candidate elected. Important to remember is that while it may seem that most people are online these days, tens of millions are not.

Allowing the candidate's online presence to intimidate or alienate those who prefer to stay out of the digital space can lead to unwanted pushback and detrimental outcomes. In addition, no political campaign can afford to neglect its primary website. Unlike social media platforms, the candidate's website is a space that the campaign has under its complete control, so this must remain updated and well trafficked.

New Ways to Engage

The uses of social media are expanding rapidly, and are limited only by the imaginations of campaign directors. Here are some of the more popular implementations:

Blog. The notion of the "blog" (derived from the words "web log") is the starting point for a great deal of social media activity. Whether the campaign designates a single person to control its social media outreach or whether several people are authorized to represent the campaign via social media, every project, meeting, decision, program, event, milepost, and activity can be mentioned in a blog that is disseminated, automatically or manually, throughout your campaign's social network (that is, through your network of social media platforms).

Build and maintain the passion. It is easy, amidst all this technology, to lose track of what drives your campaign's success. Most likely, it is a vision, a goal, and an effort that stimulate some degree of passion in the hearts and minds of your constituents, motivating them to support you. That interest and passion are central, and should never become lost in the whirl and excitement of your campaign's social media activity. It takes perspective and focus to keep social media efforts subordinate to and supportive of the campaign's broader mission.

Create more popular in-person and online events. One of the ways that social media functions effectively is to develop an audience and keep this group apprised of the latest doings they're likely to care about. Campaigns that work the social media space effectively can leverage this feature to attract more participation in their milestone events. They can also utilize Internet technology to create new events—webinars, online meetings, interactive activities, and so forth—events that wouldn't otherwise be practical from a budgetary or logistical standpoint.

Get to know your audience better. One of the most powerful promises of social media is the potential to know your constituents and stakeholders in more depth and detail. Familiarity with social media technology allows you to combine what you already know about people associated with your campaign or candidate (their names, their email addresses, perhaps their physical addresses, and more) with a great deal of additional information they readily provide about themselves through their online activities.

You can use various social media analysis tools to find out more (in the aggregate) about their interests, their activities, what media they consume, how they spend their time, even where they shop and what they buy, all of which play important roles in your candidate's targeting and positioning. Various tracking tools and social media measurement tools allow you to research how people are finding and using your online information. As you unlock these details, you can begin to optimize your online presence to increase your audience and your supporters.

Invite participation. In the old days, campaigns invited potential supporters to make contact by including a telephone number for campaign headquarters in core communications. That still works. But now, this is augmented by technologies that allow people to make their first contact with your campaign or candidate by texting a message or posting on a web page. For example, a simple invitation on your website, your outbound emails, your car, your t-shirt, or your exhibition booth—something along the lines of, "Text to *555555* with your name to be notified of upcoming events in your area"—makes an extremely attractive and powerful outreach tool.

Make tools and resources available. Social media helps to more widely disseminate information about your campaign, so it makes sense to augment your social media efforts by providing online tools and resources—including donation forms, printable brochures, flyers, posters, and more—right where people in your social network can easily find them. It takes a little time, money, and technological know-how to create these online resources, or digitize their offline counterparts, but they facilitate greater involvement. Because social media supports the rapid distribution of graphics, audio, and video, certain platforms can also help to ensure that every potential spokesperson in your campaign stays on message.

Post photos and videos online. People enjoy looking at visual material, and they tend to enjoy it even more when they see themselves and people they know. Today it is easy and inexpensive to take thousands of photos and shoot reams of video at every gathering, and then post the best bits online. "Tagging" people in these photos and videos alerts your social network to the presence of these materials, and generally draws an online crowd. Social media tools then make it easy for people who see these materials to share them with others they know. Pretty soon, your photo or video has gained some viral momentum, and your message begins reaching people who otherwise might never learn about your candidate.

One item to note: You may wish to provide a note indicating how photos and video might be used within your social networks so that participants are aware ahead of time, and any individuals wishing to avoid this can opt out. In essence, this functions a bit like the media release, which ensures against backlash from individuals who are featured. Remember, the goal is to create community, not unhappy voters.

Post your location(s) online. New technology now allows those who feel comfortable with social media to share and respond to details of their whereabouts and about specific venues nearby. The next time your campaign holds an event, for example, you can use location-based technology, such as Foursquare or Facebook Places to let people know where you are and what you are doing. People who monitor this type of content (which synchs up with all of the major social networks) will be able to drop by and participate.

You can also create a location-based online presence for your campaign, essentially posting the name, address, and contact information in an online database that makes your campaign available based on location. By attaching a descriptive tag, you'll attract people who are looking to support campaign activities in their area. Within these same databases, people will also be able to document their attendance at your events, which has the effect of immediately advising everyone in their personal social networks about your candidate and its campaign activities.

Recycle media mentions. Creating online "alerts" that bring you links to media mentions of your candidate will generally provide a fair amount of fodder for social media outreach. It is easy to recycle these news stories, blog items, links to your web pages, and other online references by sharing them through your social networks. This not only helps keep your candidate top of mind.

Tell your story. Many campaigns use social media to replicate their offline fundraising activities. They ask for support in the same old ways, but now they do it with blogs and tweets, rather than direct mailings and telephone solicitations. That's a big mistake. Social media represents a new communications paradigm, which requires a new messaging construct. With virtually unlimited online pages, you call tell your supporters and potential supporters a great deal about what's going on inside the campaign, as well as who's working on various initiatives, the progress to date, next steps, and how supporters can get involved.

The more you reveal through social media about the candidates and activities within the campaign, the more points of interest you are providing to which your constituents can respond. You'll want to use social media to magnify your impact on supporters when and where it counts most (e.g., just after announcing your candidate will run). You can also use social media during "quiet phases" when a run is still being considered, in an effort to build a larger, stronger community and position your candidate to reap bigger rewards when you once again turn up the heat on your fundraising efforts at key points in the campaign.

Maximize the native opportunity. It is hard not to notice that younger people are naturally drawn to today's most advanced technologies. In part, this is the differential between the "natives" (those who have grown up with social media) and the "immigrants" (those who have migrated to these sites). While the age demographic continues to skew upward, still, campaigns can take advantage of the affinity for social media of younger generations by utilizing technology to support more of their decision-making, activities, and overall presence. The inevitable result will be more opportunities for young people to get involved, have an impact, and accept volunteer roles within the campaign.

That said, campaigns would be remiss in ignoring the "immigrants" who are generally comprised of people over the age of 30. Keep in mind that the online space is about value. Hence, we are seeing more and more seniors signing on to social networks, and accessing web sites for critical information on topics of importance to them, including health-care reform, social security, and more.

The takeaway: Target content appropriately for each demographic, but avoid discounting any demographic when it comes to social networks.

Indeed, the power of social media for the political campaign is its ability to engage target demographics in a concentrated way. In addition, social media serves as the great neutralizer between the campaign haves and have-nots. When used properly, social media can give a bare-bones campaign with the well-lined pockets.

1 Amash,J. (2010, 24 December). https://www.facebook.com/justinamash

2 *Social media and politics in 2010 campaign.* n.d. Web. (2011, 27 January) http://www.pewinternet.org/Press-Releases/2011/Politics-and-Social-Media.aspx.

3 *Social media and politics in 2010.*

4 *Political Campaigns and social media.* n.d. Web. (2010, 25 October). http://www.c-spanvideo.org/program/296202-1.

5 Lee, C. E. (2011, 14 March) Donors Told Obama in Weaker Position. *The Wall Street Journal.* http://online.wsj.com/article/SB10001424052748704893604576198511568155224.html?mod=googlenews_wsj

CHAPTER 2

Campaign Planning

I N THE LAST 10 YEARS, digital political campaigns—with slick websites, efficient fundraising tools and thriving online communities—have evolved from nice-to-have novelties to the backbone of successful runs for office.

As is the case with any tactic or effort used in political campaigns, using online elements as part of your election strategy also entails a great deal of planning. Unlike an individual business owner or large corporation using digital strategies including social media, politicians seeking office have a different set of challenges. Those include an opposing candidate as well as the interest group or party, which is always part of the mix and ready to question, challenge or confront any element that might make you less palatable to the voters. While competition clearly exists in business, it is enacted in a way that is far less direct and swift (e.g., we won't see Coca-Cola offering an attack ad against Pepsi for a new product launch or vice versa). Still, the goal for business and politics is largely the same—to create strong name recognition (branding), build a strong community of support, and generate revenue.

Understanding that the state of social media remains relatively young, and that new networks, platforms, software and apps appear every day, the following outlines the basics for building a solid foundational plan designed to offer a distinct advantage for any campaign, with an eye toward adding new elements as the campaign develops and as social network and its users continue to evolve.

Create an online presence. One of the first places the average person turns for information on politicians (or anything or anyone for that matter) is the Internet. This means the first stop for any political campaign is the building of a strong online presence with a website (including web elements designed specifically for mobile web browsing), a blog, a Facebook fan page, Twitter account, a LinkedIn profile and any other social media networks where constituents are present in large numbers. When you create these platforms, you are also in better control of the messages disseminating about the politician and are becoming part of the conversations that are taking place, with or without someone working on the campaign being involved. When you're creating your online presence, be sure to remember that the campaign message should be at the forefront and remain the focal point in all activity—be it online in your emails, social media profile page or Twitter messages to your direct-mail pieces and in-person appearances. All of these platforms can have a donation button, or ask, which allows visitors to the platform to give as much as they want, when they want.

Identify power partners. Just as politicians align themselves with other candidates and groups in the real world, the same alignment can and should take place online. This can include family members and friends of the politician who are online and active in these social media networks. It can also include enlisting online groups. When assembling online support, these individuals and groups can become the biggest supporters and allies because they can use their own social media profiles and groups to disseminate information and conjure up additional supporters. It is akin to assembling your own cheerleading squad. According to ABC News, an individual is capable of raising hundreds of thousands of dollars by simply tapping into their own social networks.

For example, Brian Shortsleeve reached out to his social media network to raise $100,000 for the Republican gubernatorial candidate Charles Baker in Massachusetts. Five months into his campaign, Baker has raised $1.6 million in campaign funds and by the end of 2009 raised a total of $2.3 million, which was more than double that of his opponent in the campaign.

For example, for New York State Senator Kemp Hannon, Legislative Aide Nicole Russo says, "Our goal by using social media is to have an active conversation with our constituents. Sometimes we have to ask the hard questions and get real, truthful, and sometimes harsh answers. The more we know about what our constituents are thinking, the better we can serve them."[1]

Russo says Facebook has proven to be the most effective tool in communicating with the Senator's audience. Russo says Facebook has become "almost a personal news outlet for both Senator Hannon, the community and the state" because constituents can find information on key issues of the district and voice their own opinions all on the Facebook page.

Approaching fundraising using social media, where constituents turn into fundraisers for the political candidate, relieves the campaign staff from having to ask continuously for more and more donations. Instead the word spreads like wildfire, without the candidate's office having to proactively seek it.

Use Facebook, Twitter and other social media networks. Facebook has surpassed Google as the number one sharing website, which means that it is the number one place on which every politician should have a platform. Twitter is the leader in information and message dissemination, which is the best way for political messages to have an impact. At a minimum, politicians should be using these two networks as part of their political campaign fundraising efforts. When you are building these social media profiles, pages, and networks, consistency is the key. Make sure the look and feel of your social media efforts match the look and feel of your website, direct mail pieces, and other campaign efforts.

Representative Amash noted, "I wasn't considering a run for Congress or any other seat when I began posting my votes, but Facebook has turned into a fantastic campaigning tool. Above all, it has helped me to gain credibility with voters. When I say that I'm a principled, consistent conservative, people know that it is true. They can see it, and they can tell from our discussions that I'm actually reading the bills. Because I'm willing to explain myself and account for my actions, I've gained Facebook fans from across the political spectrum. Some of my best interactions are with people who disagree with my votes. I'm trying to foster the kind of civil, rational discourse that has been missing from politics for a long time."[2]

Be engaged. The key to effective use of social media in political campaigns is that the politician and his staff are fully engaged in the effort. Social media is about more than shooting messages out in the online world. Not only is social media an effective tool for dissemination, but it is also highly effective in "listening" to what your audience is saying. You can monitor what your supporters are saying, as well as what your opponents have to say. Social media provides a fast and efficient feedback loop so you have a finger on the pulse of sentiment. Engagement is also about sharing news stories, connecting with your constituents, answering questions, and responding to their comments.

According to Amash, he is the one who is engaged with his audience, rather than allowing a staff member to handle the interaction on his behalf. Amash says he is the person who is posting the updates, making comments, and replying to the questions and comments left by his followers. "In fact, as of now, no one else—not even my legislative staff or campaign staff—has access to it. Yes, it's a lot of work, but it's important that I hear directly from constituents and that they hear directly from me."

Social media use should not replace other campaigning efforts. Instead, social media efforts should enhance the other efforts of political campaigning. This means raising money for the campaign will still involve direct mail, in-person grassroots campaigning, candidate travel, along with social media tools such as Facebook, Twitter, and YouTube.

The Distinction Between Your Social Media Campaign and Your Social Media Strategy. The first stop in using social media as part of a political campaign strategy is to understand the difference between a social media campaign and a social media strategy. The social media strategy is the horse, while the social media campaign is the cart. You want to put the horse before the cart. In essence, social media strategy involves creating the plan for how you are going to use social media campaigns to engage the community.

Once you have a full understanding of who you are talking to with your social media efforts and what you are going to say, then you can create a social media campaign. The campaign involves providing useful information that your audience seeks. It is a mistake to create a social media campaign without taking the time to first implement a social media strategy. This would be akin to a doctor writing you a prescription without first diagnosing what is causing the symptoms you have.

Why Social Media Matters in Political Campaigns. Social media is in widespread use, so more voters are using social media networks to find information on politicians and to become involved in the political process. Since this is where more and more voters are turning for information, it means that more politicians need to be where their voters are. With a growing population on Facebook, politicians can use the tools built into social media networks such as Facebook to not only find their audience, but also to engage them in ways that effectively help the candidate to win the election in an efficient and cost-effective way.

According to Julielyn Gibbons, President of i3 Strategies, an online strategy consulting firm, and Senior Fellow at the New Organizing Institute in Washington, DC, "Some of the tactics that we used included asking supporters to change their Facebook profile picture and Twitter avatar to the campaign logo days before the election, posting and sharing campaign ads and messages on YouTube, encouraging supporters to share on their Facebook walls, [and] creating and spreading a hashtag when folks tweeted about the campaign." Gibbons also shares that integration of social media networks is the key to a successful political campaign. "Every outlet linked to or mentioned the other outlets. For instance, at the end of every YouTube video, we included the URL of the campaign website, the Facebook page, and the Twitter page. Tweets linked to YouTube videos, important updates on the Facebook Page, links to fundraising pages on the site, etc."

The quantity of content in social media campaigning is not the endgame either. It is more important to understand where people are finding information on the campaign than it is to assume that they are finding the information using any particular outlet.

Consider the California Governor race between Jerry Brown (D) and Meg Whitman (R). When you analyze online and other types of data, you can find that before the first three debates in the campaign took place, the websites that were the most influential in the campaign included one where Bill Clinton was endorsing Brown; a Whitman advertisement that showed a clip of Clinton attacking Brown; and the fact that Whitman set a record on the amount of money she invested in her campaign.

The three debates between the two candidates unfolded between September 28 and October 12, 2010. Not only did these three weeks hold the debates, but some scandals emerged as well. After this three-week period, influential websites changed. Now the three most influential sites included one of Brown's associates referring to Whitman as a whore, Whitman offering to take a lie detector test to prove she didn't know her housekeeper was an illegal immigrant, and a recap of the issues covered in the October 12 debate.

While the Obama campaign may have inaugurated the full-blown use of social media in political campaigns, other political campaigns have certainly taken notice of the positive effects it can have on fundraising efforts—and winning the race. Text messages, Twitter, Facebook and other social media platforms have proven to be effective and successful in creating political outcomes where candidates raise the money they need for their campaigns and to ultimately win the election.

Treating the online aspect of a campaign with the utmost seriousness, then integrating it with offline operations, was one of the keys to Barack Obama's victory in 2008. On personnel alone, Obama's campaign boasted a 10-to-1 advantage in online staff, compared to McCain's.

When the numbers were crunched after election day, they revealed that Obama supporters working online organized 200,000 real-world events, formed 35,000 virtual communities, wrote 400,000 blog posts, generated 14.5 million "television viewing hours" on YouTube, and raised $30 million on 70,000 personal fundraising pages.[3]

It is true that John McCain was the first presidential candidate to raise 1 million dollars online (back in 2000), while Howard Dean in 2004 and Ron Paul in 2008 energized armies of boosters.

However, the Obama campaign was the first to combine online fundraising acumen, organizational discipline, organic community building, and "buzz" generation.

As a result, unlike candidates whose digital experiments paved the way, Obama actually won his race.

A post campaign case study by Edelman[4] observed:

"Obama's campaign started early, was built to scale, brought in the right team, and struck a difficult balance between inspiring the kinetic energy of a movement and channeling the enthusiasm into the precise activities that are needed to win a campaign— donations, organization, and getting out the vote—in the specific neighborhoods, districts, and states that the campaign needed to win.

"It ultimately used the same tools that many campaigns had previously employed. However, the campaign did everything incrementally better than its competitors. The Obama campaign leveraged all the tools of social media to give ordinary Americans access to resources usually reserved for professional campaign operatives. His operation was cycles ahead."

Of course, the Obama campaign had a little help from powerful, plugged-in friends such as Netscape founder and Facebook board member Marc Andreessen. Few political candidates have Obama's impressive Rolodex or massive war chest. However, the same basic tools and tactics can be used by anyone, with the added advantage that these presidential hopefuls spent millions of dollars and hours testing them—so you don't have to.

The good news is, campaign managers will now face fewer fights about "wasting money on that web stuff." The bad news is that, while online campaign tools are fairly simple to use, employing them *correctly* demands strategic planning and expert execution.

Build A Nimble Infrastructure

Today's sophisticated voters demand a mutually respectful relationship with a candidate, and expect to be treated as more than just an "X" on a ballot or a signature on a check. Online campaigning nurtures that relationship thanks to its ease of use, immediacy, and ability to sustain one-to-one communication.

In order to stand a chance of succeeding, even a local political campaign should have these basic elements in place online:

- A website that serves as the campaign's online "headquarters"
- Constituent Relations Management software with integrated email functionality
- Social media and networking presences: Facebook, Twitter, Flickr, and other popular and/or relevant sites
- Online fundraising strategies
- Use of text messaging and mobile phone apps

Tying all these elements together is the job of a designated staffer. Obama and other victorious candidates all hired new media experts to run their online campaigns— individuals who reported directly to the campaign manager and were far more than just techies setting up web sites. Ideally, such individuals combine expertise in marketing, communications, promotion, *and* technology. The staffer "who knows how to fix computers" is no more qualified for this particular job than a copy-machine repairman is qualified to be a professional speechwriter.

Establish Your Website

Every campaign needs an easy-to-navigate, uncluttered, informative website that makes it instantly obvious to visitors how to donate, volunteer, sign up for email, RSS feeds and other alerts, and learn about the candidate's background and beliefs.

A short welcome video starring the candidate is now considered de rigueur. Ideally, the site offers templates for letters to the editor, "tell-a-friend" emails and other engagement tools.

Note: a Facebook "profile" or "fan" page does NOT count as your main site. More on that below.

This main website is the campaign's online hub, inviting visitors to connect with the campaign on social media networks such as Twitter, Facebook, LinkedIn and more. In turn, each of the candidate's social media accounts directs users back to that main online hub.

Encourage supporter involvement at various levels. Not everybody will be inspired to enter a "campaign commercial" contest, but many will happily vote for their favorite entry with a simple click.

The days of having the campaign manager's teenage nephew build a rudimentary website are over. For voters and journalists—as well as for one's opponents—a campaign website IS the candidate.

These sites may not seem glamorous, but according to a study conducted after the 2010 UK general election, they were the most popular destination for voters, wielding far more influence than YouTube and Twitter.[5]

In terms of backend, this site must be easy for trusted staff members to update. Breaking news and dramatic developments can't wait for a freelancer or a high-priced designer to answer an urgent text message. Build and maintain the site using a proven, intuitive content management system (CMS), not just raw HTML or a vendor's private label CMS.

Consultants Steve Pearson and Ford O'Connell advise campaigners to "talk to several vendors [and] look at a variety of options. Plan to spend $3,000 to $5,000. You can spend more, but it's not necessary unless you have a specialized digital campaign plan. Avoid wasting your time and money building a digital black hole."[6]

(And it should go without saying by now: print your website's URL on all print collateral. Using a free service such as LinkedTube, you can even "brand" clickable hyperlinks right onto your videos.)

Add Constituent Relations and Email Management

Constituent Relations Management (CRM) software is widely available and affordable, especially when compared to the man hours otherwise spent (inefficiently) entering supporter information into a spreadsheet program, then doing mail merges using yet another, possibly incompatible, software platform.

Thanks to easy-to-use automation platforms, CRM increases efficiently and accuracy exponentially. Supporters find it simple to sign up for alerts, while members of the staff receive instant data they can sort and analyze in seconds. That's why smart campaigns rely on robust CRM software to manage that all-important tool: email.

Despite the hype surrounding Twitter, texting, and Facebook, email is "still the most effective tool to raise money, motivate volunteers and keep supporters engaged," says Colin Delany of epolitics.com.

"For example, roughly two-thirds of the $500 million that Barack Obama raised online came directly from someone clicking on a 'donate now' button in an email message. Email reaches many people who still haven't joined the social web, for one thing, but it's also turned out in practice to have a much higher response rate than other channels, sometimes by a factor of ten or more."[7]

Delany notes that the response rate for email over Facebook or Twitter is "10 or 20 times higher for a particular ask." Why? Because most people have email at work and at home, while social networking, despite its movement toward the mainstream, is still young.

Every email message should contain an "ask." However, don't turn every email into a request for a donation. Welcome new subscribers to the list, then invite them to help promote a campaign video, come to a local event or pass along information to friends. They may not have the hang of "re-tweeting," but most subscribers will know how to forward an email. Create landing pages that match the "ask" in the email *exactly*. Don't make supporters click on links that take them to an off-message destination.

In other words: every "push" should have a corresponding "pull."

Personalization is a two-way street: along with personalizing the "to" field, all emails should be sent by a real campaign staffer, with his or her own title and "from" address.

Don't send too many messages. One exception: subscribers will understand, and even expect an increase in messages as election day draws closer.

Texas GOP Governor's Race

According to Will Franklin, Texas Governor Rick Perry's Director of New Media & Research, Perry successfully defeated Republican candidate Senator Kay Bailey Hutchison in the March 2010 primary by utilizing social media. Twitter, Flickr, Facebook, YouTube, Blip, iPhone, Android, Palm, and Craigslist were utilized.

Franklin said that Governor Perry made social media a vital part of his day-to-day leadership as governor, and a critical component of his campaign's communication strategy.

"Governor Perry avoided a runoff with Senator Hutchison not just because he had more Facebook fans or Twitter followers—numbers aren't everything—but because he personally believed in the power of social media to fundamentally reshape the way that he interacts with the people of Texas," he said. "The Perry campaign didn't view social media as an obligatory task to check off on a to-do list. Rather, social media was central to the campaign's messaging."

Perry, the 47th Governor of Texas, first assumed office in December 2000 when Governor George W. Bush resigned to become President of the United States. Perry was elected to a four-year term in 2002, and then re-elected in 2006 and in 2010.

Paul Burka of *Burka Blog* states that because Perry was like a boxer who fought a contender with a big reputation and won, he has good potential for the presidency of the United States.

Perry and his team learned the power of the social media from the 2008 presidential campaign, and put this into practice. The Perry campaign never deployed a yard sign, and never knocked on a door. He and his team built a brutally efficient political machine by relying on personal appearances and voter contact through the electronic media.

Burka, Paul. *Last words about the GOP governor's race. n.d.* Web. 4 March 2010.
http://www.texasmonthly.com/blogs/burkablog/?p=6511. March 4, 2010.
    http://en.wikipedia.org/wiki/Rick_Perry.

That subscriber list is a precious commodity. Whatever happens to the website itself post-election, make sure you walk away with those irreplaceable names and numbers when the campaign is over.

This may go without saying, but maintain a friendly, professional tone. Make a promise not to sell or trade collected contact information—and keep it. And keep your communications opt-in only: don't sign up anyone for emails, no matter who they are.

Kiss More Babies Via Social Networks

Use of social media sites such as Twitter, LinkedIn, and Facebook has skyrocketed. More than 60 percent of adults in the United States belong to a social network, but *most belong to only one.*

You will want to establish a presence on all of the networks with quantifiable traffic and activity, but avoid establishing a presence on every new network one that comes along. Be sure to feature standard Facebook and Twitter "chiclets" or link buttons on your main campaign page.

Be aware that each of these networks has its own etiquette, potential, and limitations.

Facebook estimates its U.S. users have 120 million accounts, and half of those check in at least once a day, to chat with "friends."

It is easy to obsess over how many "friends" a candidate has. If you're running a campaign for local office or the state legislature, say consultants Pearson and O'Connell, "several hundred fans might be a realistic goal; if you're running a statewide race, perhaps several thousand fans might be your goal."

Even if a candidate already has a personal Facebook profile, set up a separate campaign "page," and make that the focus. After the election, that candidate can go back to using his or her original personal page to stay in touch with family and friends. In addition, a Facebook "page" allows for multiple administrators and other features not available with ordinary profiles.

Interaction is the key, not numbers. Facebook is perfect for pushing out information about the candidate and the campaign. Adding photos is especially productive; Facebook lets users "tag" individuals who appear in photos, who will then receive a message saying they've been tagged. Few people can resist checking in to see other photos of the event they attended. (Adding a "thanks for coming" message from the candidate is a no-brainer.) Ask "friends" to "share" or "like" new additions. That's the way a Facebook account grows, and users expect it.

Facebook also has a thriving and affordable advertising system. Unlike Google Ads, this self-service tool lets you target ad placements, not by keywords, but by less esoteric criteria including location and age. "For the cost of a pizza," say Pearson and O'Connell, "you could have an ad campaign running" in minutes.

Experts advise tasking one individual with Facebook maintenance, spending a bare minimum of 20 minutes a day answering messages and putting up new material.

Every campaign also needs a Twitter account, to send out brief messages to "followers." Twitter users hate hype, puffery and self-promotion, however, so earn trust (and followers) by becoming a reliable source of useful information. If a candidate is passionate about certain issues, pass along news stories on that subject. Re-posting (aka "re-tweeting" or "RT-ing") other Twitter users' messages, with an added "Check this out!" is also a proven path to popularity.

Plus, simply adding "Please RT" to a tweet (and note, that "please" makes a difference) will send a message beyond one's existing following and encourage new signups.

To avoid losing these readers, brand every tweet with the URL of the main campaign site, using a tool such as MarketMeTweet. This site also makes it possible to schedule tweets and otherwise semi-automate a Twitter account.

Because space is at a premium in the 140-character-universe of Twitter, use shorteners to transform long website URLs into clickable snippets. Use a URL shortener (such as bit.ly or tiny.url) that keeps stats on how often tweets are clicked and forwarded. Note patterns in popularity and repeat whatever gets the best response.

While it is a tempting timesaver, many experts advise against linking Twitter and Facebook feeds. Besides creating a sometimes ugly, repetitive feedback loop, messages that make sense on one platform will appear cryptic on another. Treating all networks as separate entities pays off in the currency that is most valued among social media denizens: authenticity.

Yet another Twitter client (application) to consider is your candidate's level of Klout (http://www.Klout.com). While not the perfect quantitative measure, this Twitter tool enables you to determine, at least on some level, the degree of influence your candidate has based on an algorithm that produces a "Klout" score. This is a handy way to measure not only your candidate, but the level of influence of the people who are following your candidate on Twitter. This will enable your campaign to gauge the potential influence certain followers may have and thus, the level of effort your campaign may place on acquiring these types of followers.

A presence on Twitter and Facebook is primarily aimed at growing the campaign's email subscriber list, so gently but clearly direct "friends" and "followers" to the main campaign site.

What about blogs? Maintaining an authentic blog—one written by the candidate, featuring candid observations and updated daily—is probably impossible, not to mention unwise. And online users can spot a fake blog instantly and are unforgiving about anything inauthentic. A blog with a handful of half-hearted posts, with the last one date stamped six months earlier, is worse than no blog at all.

Hence, the more fruitful approach may be to reach out to established political bloggers in relevant districts and respectfully invite them to visit the official website, or better yet, attend an upcoming event with the candidate. There is no secret to blogger relations. Approach them as you would traditional reporters. Many bloggers are also journalists by profession, so establishing a good rapport is always smart campaign practice.

Traditional campaign managers understandably fear losing control of carefully crafted messages when setting out into the no-holds-barred environment of social media. However, studies show that peer-to-peer messaging carries more weight with recipients than exquisitely honed "professional" copy.[8]

Indeed, rather than trying to overly control the message, be prepared for inevitable controversies by having good "defensive" content visible all over the web. Make this messaging easy to find by seeding it with the keywords curious voters are searching for. Politely direct detractors on Facebook or Twitter to a new video of the candidate addressing the issue. Be sure the video's tags on YouTube are similarly seeded with relevant hot-button keywords. Inform the email list of the campaign's response so they can text talking points and forward messages to friends, families, and coworkers.

Online Fundraising Options

Piryx Fundraising estimated in June 2010 that $4 billion would be raised online during that year's U.S. election cycle—twice the record amount donated in 2008.[9]

While it is certainly possible to just stick a familiar PayPal "DONATE" button on every page of a candidate's website (and ways to donate should appear on each page, not just the main one), other tools, such as WePay and Kickstarter, are designed to address the particular fundraising needs of political campaigns.

GoFundMe, for example, is built off the PayPal platform, but enables campaigns to set up customized donation pages that include "tell-a-friend" options for Facebook, email, and Twitter. That peer-to-peer functionality was built into MyBarackObama. com and played a large role in the Democratic contender's record numbers of repeat, small donations.

By analyzing the data collected through the Constituent Relationship Management system, it becomes easier to "tailor the ask." Don't ask a first-time $10 donor for $200 the next time around; suggest $20 instead. Quite simply, don't treat supporters like bank machines.

One fundraising technique uniquely adapted to the online world is the "money bomb," in which a campaign tries to raise a large amount of money in a short period of time. Money bombs work best in an atmosphere of urgency and enthusiasm, are heavily promoted, and have a clear deadline and purpose. However, they can also, literally, bomb—and that public failure can become an embarrassment for the campaign.

Let Your Supporters Travel With You:
Text Messages and Phone Apps

Text messaging and mobile phone "apps" are emerging as new, standard-issue items in the online campaign toolbox.

For example, on election day, Obama supporters received a minimum of three text messages, prompting them to ask friends if they needed rides to polling stations.

As powerful as email is, it has also become ubiquitous, which works in its favor—and against it. Text messaging is still a relative novelty. Studies show that while email messages stack up unanswered, people with cell phones read 90 percent of their texts. Even voters without regular access to email (from low-income seniors to on-the-road salespeople, truckers, and contractors) usually have a cell phone and are regular texters.

One 2006 study found that text messages "helped increase voter turnout by 4 percent at the cost of only $1.56 per vote, whereas traditional door-to-door canvassing or phone banking" costs out to $20 to $30 a vote.[10] With the dramatic rise in mobile-device ownership and usage, we should expect these numbers to rise.

"Text messaging was the tool that we used to have a dramatic impact on talk radio," notes Rob Willington, new media director for current U.S. Senator from Massachusetts Scott Brown, who famously won Ted Kennedy's seat for the Republicans in 2009.[11]

"We sent text messages with the call-in number of the talk shows," explained Willington. "Talk radio is such an old medium, but when we combine that old medium with a new medium, it became very powerful stuff."

The Brown campaign also developed a GPS based "Android/iPhone/BlackBerry walk app because it sped up the process" of door-to-door campaigning.

"We launched the application on Sunday, and on Sunday, Monday and Tuesday we were able to get people out of our offices quicker," says Willington. "The app shows volunteers the nearest house to visit, directions to get there, and talking points to use during the conversation."

The information gathered door to door was entered right on the mobile device and went right into the campaign's data files. No more extra work filling out and remembering to turn in paper forms!

The Obama campaign also released an iPhone app that pinpointed local events, contacted staffers, read news releases, and facilitated monetary donations.

Of course, online campaign innovation isn't restricted to the United States, and its particular problems and solutions are universal. After the 2010 presidential election in Sri Lanka, one analyst dismissed a candidate's online campaign in terms that may sound familiar:

"His campaign team is everywhere online, but they don't mobilize voters and organize communities. They don't build a consensual database of mobile numbers by promising that in return, supporters would get campaign news before the media."

Another candidate "confined himself to an amateur website and a few Facebook ads" which showed "one's capacity—or the lack of it."[12]

Sheer imitation doesn't always breed success, however. Dr. Ashraf Ghani reportedly "Obama-ized" his 2009 presidential campaign, gathering thousands of Facebook friends, whereas incumbent (and the eventual winner) President Karzai "had no online campaign to speak of."[13]

The jury is still out on whether Benigno "Noynoy" Aquino's 700,000 Facebook friends helped make him President of the

Philippines in 2010, as opposed to his famous last name—or a combination of both factors and countless others.[14]

Wherever a candidate is running, one thing is certain: online campaigning does not replace traditional tactics, but it is now a staple ingredient for any candidate who hopes to win an election.

1 Densley, R. (2011, February 22). "Canadian Government Joins US and Europe—Allows Social Media into Commons." *The iStrategy Blog*. Blog post retrieved from http://www.istrategyconference.com/blog/?category=Social-Media&title=Canadian-government-joins-US-and-Europe---allows-social-media-into-commons&pid=226

2 McKnight, R. (2011, March 24). The Power of Social Media in Politics. Blog post retrieved from http://www.racknine.com/blog/social-media/power-social-media-politics/

3 Stanton, J. (2009, 20 April) The Man Behind Obama's Online Election Campaign. *Digital Communities*. http://www.digitalcommunitiesblogs.com/web_20_convergence/2009/04/the-man-behind-obamas-online-e.php

4 Edelman, R. Web. n.d. The Social Pulpit: Barack Obama's Social Media Toolkit. (2009) http://www.scribd.com/doc/10928356/Social-Pulpit-Barack-Obamas-Social-Media-Toolkit

5 Vincent, M. New Kid on the Block Brings in Business. *Financial Times*. (2010, 11 June) http://www.ft.com/intl/cms/s/0/28448dcc-7362-11df-ae73-00144feabdc0.html#axzz1T09CLuzm

6 Pearson, S and O'Connell, F. "Down Home Digital: Keep Your Digital Bandwagon Out of the Ditch." *Campaigns & Elections*. (2010 1 April) http://www.politicsmagazine.com/magazine-issues/april-2010/keep-your-digital-bandwagon-out-of-the-ditch

7 Delany, C. (2009, September 28). Winning Online in 2010: Tools, Time and Resources. *epolitics.com*. Blog post retrieved from http://www.epolitics.com/2009/09/28/winning-online-in-2010-part-two-tools-time-and-resources/

8 Edelman, R.

9 "Fundraising Tool Piryx Projects $4B In Online Political Donations For 2010 Election Cycle." *TechCrunch*. (2010, 25 June) http://techcrunch.com/2010/06/25/fundraising-tool-piryx-projects-4b-in-online-political-donations-for-2010-election-cycle/

10 "How To Find & Mobilize Young Voters II." CompleteCampaigns.com. n.d. Web http://www.completecampaigns.com/article.asp?articleid=118

11 ClickZ.com. *Digital Campaigns 101*. (2010) http://www.scribd.com/doc/32938238/null

12 "Sri Lankan Presidential Election: Social Media in Election Reporting." *Global Voices*. (2010, 25 January) http://globalvoicesonline.org/2010/01/25/sri-lankan-presidential-election-social-media-in-election-reporting

13 "Afghan Presidential Candidate Obama-izes His Campaign." *techPresident*. (2009, 17 July) http://techpresident.com/blog-entry/afghan-presidential-candidate-obama-izes-his-campaign

14 Corporal, L Lee. "Philippines Presidential Campaign Thrives in Online World." *The Irrawaddy*. (2010, 22 February) http://www.irrawaddy.org/article.php?art_id=17858

CHAPTER 3

Talent Revolution—Building the New Campaign Team

TODAY'S CAMPAIGN TEAMS look dramatically different from the teams of even five years ago. With the importance of social media as a viable means of harnessing voter engagement and support, anyone involved with a political campaign should be taking a new approach to his or her campaign team. This section highlights what a political campaign team used to be comprised of, as well as the skills sets and campaign positions that should comprise a social media enabled campaign.

In part, the team will be based on the content strategy, but campaigns must spend their efforts securing the ideal hires (those who will work directly on social media, and those will work outside of the social media space—but who will be strategizing, organizing events, and pitching to the media.

This, by no means, threatens to dethrone the longtime campaign masters, but it does mean that if the masters are not up to speed on new platforms themselves, they'll need to know enough to hire staffers who are.

Holding rallies, appearing at schools or knocking on doors are still important methods for gaining votes, but these methods have to include an online element for success. This trend began in 2004 with Howard Dean's online organizing efforts on MeetUp.org and the Fifty-State Strategy. That was the first time a candidate worked to establish a campaign presence in every state. The online movement also included the sophisticated statistical micro-targeting of voters devised by Alexander Gage during President George W. Bush's 2004 reelection campaign. Dean's efforts included raising $50 million online—a noble feat considering his average campaign donation was $80.

In comparison, Bush's team reached out to 92 percent of potential voters in Iowa and 84 percent in Florida, which increased dramatically from the 50 percent reached in the 2000 election.

Part of this online movement, MoveOn.org, introduced another key element to online campaign strategy—online phone banking. Rahaf Harfoush discusses in her recap on the Obama campaign[1] that by allowing visitors to call on behalf of a political topic such as going to vote, and addressing issues, MoveOn.org enabled phone banking to move from behind the campaign scenes to the masses.

These strategies were beneficial to national campaigns in 2004 and forward, but they were not the defining moments for Bush or Dean. Bush still relied on old strategies, but backed them with micro-targeting to create customized messaging for direct mail, calling, and events. His campaign also used a traditional tactic of reaching the conservative base and ditching the "compassionate conservative" platform they ran with in 2000. Dean was successful in establishing the campaign presence in 50 states with the online fundraising, but he could not marry his online and offline efforts.

In 2007, a junior Illinois senator named Barack Obama, put together a team that leveraged the technological and organizing successes explored by the Bush and Dean campaigns and linked them to his background in community organizing and the efforts MoveOn.org had created online to create a new era in campaigning. By implementing new media—social networking, highly targeted e-mail marketing, online fundraising, and online phone banking alongside traditional, grassroots organizing, the Obama campaign for the 2008 presidential election changed the way politicians communicate with voters.

This campaign reached voters on an entirely new level—from the ground up—and spurred the need for a talent revolution in who runs the political campaigns of the future. Today and moving forward, getting the word out is not just about sending press releases, organizing photo opportunities, or operating a phone station. The new political campaign has a multifaceted, strategic plan for reaching out to people wherever they are.

Harfoush also details how social networking and taking the campaign online requires a highly specialized team—one that is capable of testing, listening and comprehending complex data analysis on a national level. The political campaign of the future must depend on feeling the pulse of the public through online channels.

A Snapshot of Your New Media Team

The new media team for a political campaign can span an entire office floor of specialized managers and tactical implementers, or be limited to just a few people. Staffing levels depend on how large the campaign manager plans to take online efforts to reach voters. A national presidential campaign will obviously encompass a large group and multiple headquarters of new media talent, but the smaller campaign such as a state or even local candidate can benefit from learning the inside story of how this movement began.

The Obama campaign kicked off the social strategy by giving voters a home base of "getting to know the candidate" through his campaign website www.barackobama.com. Right after he announced his candidacy, the campaign team released a revamped version of the site, which featured an official blog, a campaign schedule, a video channel and a social network called www.mybarackobama.com. The launch was so successful that more than 1,000 online groups had organized using the site's tools within 24 hours of the announcement.[2]

The blog, notes Harfoush, was focused on introducing the junior senator from Chicago, but it was also a way for supporters to understand the campaign message and to serve as a "digital meet and greet."[3] They did this in two ways. Posts from staff including new media director, Joe Rospars, gave an inside view of the campaign operations and solidified the campaign message that it was more important to engage people than focus on dollars raised.

Finding the Talent Pool

In addition to the blog, the senator's Facebook presence was growing by the thousands. This is where the lessons on hiring truly begin in Obama's campaign strategy.

When she heard that the senator's presidential race was a real possibility, Meredith Segal, a student at Bowdoin College organized a Facebook group in support of the campaign. This group, Students for Barack Obama, grew to 80 chapters and 62,000 members by the time that the senator announced his candidacy. Members of the group organized into a Political Action Committee (PAC) and became the official student organization of the campaign, with Segal named the executive director.

Under her leadership, the PAC's presence grew to over 550 campus chapters and introduced high school representatives from all 50 states. This group became one of the campaign's most influential groups with 19,000 events, 406,000 phone calls, 4,500 door knocks and $1.7 million in funds raised.[4]

Hiring Lesson: Look to successful online supporters of your cause for talent.

Understanding the Audience Motivations

Rospars' strategy contains an important hiring lesson in how the team managed the online community for the Obama campaign. This team didn't just preach engaging with supporters through the words of the blog—they also did it via blog comments and other online communities.

By offering quality incentives, they were able to activate supporters. One such example is featuring milestone donors— Rashed, an IT help desk specialist from Long Beach, CA was the 75,000th donor with a five-dollar donation. They featured him on the blog in an interview. Angela, the 250,000th donor who gave just $100 was honored with a personal phone call with the senator.

Hiring Lesson: Understanding how the audience wants to be recognized is an important characteristic for campaign hires.

Creativity Matters

Thinking of ways to offer incentives doesn't just have to be about recognizing the nth donor; it can also be recognizing a supporter's opinion—such as when all three candidates—John McCain, Hillary Clinton and Obama—were asked to participate in a promotion with Yahoo.com's Answers community.

Clinton asked a question that received 38,000 responses and asked the community to vote for the best answer. She responded to the support on her blog. McCain asked a question that received 16,000 responses and responded with a campaign promise to reduce wasteful spending in Washington. Obama asked a question that received 17,000 responses, and the campaign team selected the best answer to the question. Then, they took the response offline by having the senator call the respondent. They recorded the call and featured it in his blog.

Hiring Lesson: Selecting staffers who think and demonstrate acumen along the lines of networking the networks, and leveraging content vital to the campaign.

Election 2008: The First Social Media Presidential Campaign

Social media was Barack Obama's not-so-secret weapon in getting elected the 44th president of the United States. He participated in Q&As with YouTube users, had nearly 4 million followers on Twitter and more than eight million fans on Facebook.

Chris Hughes, the architect behind mybarackobama.com, said that the Internet served as "the connective tissue" that helped supporters, volunteers, and campaign workers coordinate their offline and online activities.

According to Stirland, "Volunteers used Obama's website to organize a thousand phone-banking events in the last week of the race—and 150,000 other campaign-related events over the course of the campaign. Supporters created more than 35,000 groups organized by affinities like geographical proximity and shared pop-cultural interests. By the end of the campaign, myBarackObama.

com chalked up some 1.5 million accounts. And Obama raised a record-breaking $600 million in contributions from more than 3 million people, many of whom donated through the web."

Since the 1930s when Franklin Delano Roosevelt utilized the new medium of radio, presidents have explored and conquered new media. In January 1955, President Dwight D. Eisenhower held the first televised press conference. Harry Truman was the first president to have a television in the White House, and John F. Kennedy successfully navigated the quirks of the television camera. But Ronald Reagan mastered the new medium and was called the "great communicator." In 1992, Bill Clinton used non-traditional television venues by playing the saxophone on Arsenio Hall and appearing on MTV.

Macon Phillips spearheaded the design of Obama's presidential campaign website and presently serves as White House director of new media. Phillips remarked that the new media team has really tried to develop content and capacities to reach people as they shift their news habits.

"We're trying out a lot of new things, and the ultimate goal is to make sure the American public has more information about their government," Phillips said.

Fagel, Mari. *"Obama, Social Media, and Presidential Advances in Communication Technology."* Politicsdaily.com. *http://www.politicsdaily.com/2010/05/09/is-obama-using-social-media-to-bypass-the-press-corps/.* Web. 4 June 2010. *http://globalhumancapital.org/?p=216.* *http://www.wired.com/threatlevel/2008/11/propelled-by-in/comment-page-5/.*

The go point is finding your new media communications director. According to Jenifer Daniels, a political communications manager and blogger from Charlotte, North Carolina, the best political campaign team starts with communications directors who understand social media the same as they understand public relations and marketing.

She also recommends hiring a social media specialist and a web specialist to implement and manage the web technologies.

Hiring Lesson: Anyone hired to handle social media interactions or advertising should understand how to demonstrate value in the candidate and how this ties with the marketing spend—"When I can invest $1,000 in a Facebook advertising campaign and receive 2 million views, I can prove it's more valuable than spending $5,000 on kicker cards mailed to only 30,000 people," Daniels said.

Recruiting Grassroots Volunteers Online

As the Iowa caucuses approached in 2008, the Obama campaign began seeking support "on the ground" to drive voter registration and support for the candidate at the neighborhood level. Instead of using the local grapevine, they married community organizing with an online push for precinct captains. Existing precinct captain testimonials were featured on the blog and in e-mail communications. By featuring real people, the team brought the campaign message of "engage people" to its recruiting efforts.

Daniels suggests that anyone working on a political campaign needs to understand how tools such as email or text messages, which were sent daily by the Obama campaign, fit into an overall marketing strategy. "Many are drawn to the idea of using social media solely because of the experiences they had in the recent presidential election. They remember receiving text messages daily; but what they may not know is that the 140-character message started as a bound book titled *The Plan: Barack Obama's Promise to America and His Plan for the Economy, Iraq, Healthcare, and More.*"

Hiring Lesson: Identifying staffers who understand how to synch the messaging strategy means finding professionals with the right backgrounds and skills for the new political communications team.

Transparency in Communications

After a startling loss in the New Hampshire primary, the Obama campaign had to refocus the troops. The campaign again turned to transparency and online mechanisms to relay the message that it was in a tough fight against Clinton. Campaign manager, David Plouffe, wrote an email detailing where the campaign stood on fundraising, supporters, and plans for the upcoming primaries. The email, which was generated to read like an internal memo, was so well received that the campaign would use the format for upcoming efforts.

Transparency in communications is particularly important to social media users. On the local level, one former candidate, Dana Marie Kennedy, who made a run for the Phoenix City Council, said that her team of all volunteers "created a buzz with social media that showed we were a real campaign."

Her team was able to run the campaign in real time by using mobile technologies—Facebook applications for iPhone and BlackBerry. Kennedy's campaign team also planned weekly communications via email and Facebook. Plus, she had a team dedicated to Google alerts and responding to blogs and articles. At any level, social media is an important tool in organizing voters.

Hiring Lesson: Campaign staff should be comfortable with running a public-facing operation.

Social Media as a Recruitment Tool

Kennedy uses social media as a recruiting tool for Emerge America—a nonprofit organization that teaches Democratic women how to run for office.

"For the recruitment of potential Emerge applicants, social media does help," Kennedy said. "The research shows that women need to be recruited to run for office and they need to be asked multiple times. Social media is a soft ask and it plants the seed."

The Obama campaign took similar action in recruiting candidates to its Fellowship Program. This unpaid program ran for six weeks and created a team of 3,600 fellows who were divided across the country to manage phone banking, voter registration, and community organizing, among other duties. All fellows were trained in using the online tools the campaign used to organize voters and volunteers. Again, the campaign communications team featured these fellows in their online efforts including the blog and email communications.

Hiring Lesson: Reaching out to potential political social media and communication hires via social media can lead to success because it targets those who are already functioning at a higher level in this space.

Creating a Candidate's Brand—A Layered Communication Approach

Kennedy also credits social media for giving her unknown face a presence in her city council election. "In order to win the support of voters, you have to communicate with them where they are," Kennedy said. "I used my website, blog, emails, Facebook, Twitter, phone calls, and knocking on doors."

She entered the race in June of the election year, forced a sitting city council member into a run-off, and garnered 44 percent of the vote with only a volunteer staff. Even though she lost the runoff, Kennedy credits social media as a key to her success in a close race.

In addition to running for office, Kennedy was the communications director for the Hillary Clinton for President

Phoenix office. She had a volunteer staff and they used social media to push article links and Clinton's position on issues. In addition, this unpaid staff recruited additional volunteers through online channels.

Kennedy reinforces the need for a layered approach to political communications as illustrated by the Obama campaign strategy success.

Hiring Lesson: Look for professionals who understand how to grow a candidate's brand through multiple channels.

Hiring for the Audience—Look for Writers Who Get It

The Obama campaign's head of email and fundraising, Stephen Geer, took a new approach to political communications by losing the political formality and writing to the level of the audience. His team kept messaging simple and used the language that the candidate typically spoke throughout email and fundraising communications. Geer was able to keep messages short and include the overall campaign message of "respect, empower, and include."

Hiring Lesson: Identifying communications professionals who understand email marketing and writing to the audience is an important part of developing the communications team.

Hire Team Players

Molly Claflin, a national blog assistant editor for the Obama campaign, remarked on the importance of being able to communicate across teams.

"Most of us had never been involved in a national campaign before," she said. "We had to learn together. So the team email guys would ask me for help wording sentences. I would ask the ad team to help me choose the most compelling stories for the blog. Ads would ask Email which ad design layout was best. And so on. I liked the fact that though we had a job to do, we helped each other on a daily basis."[5]

Hiring Lesson: Be sure potential hires thrive in a team environment.

Entertain Proposals from Interested Parties

Early in the Obama campaign, Kate Albright-Hanna, an Emmy-winning producer with a past working in politics approached Joe Rospars, the campaign's new media director, on composing a documentary on the campaign. When she discovered that the campaign was producing its own video content, conversations turned into an opportunity for Albright-Hanna to work full-time for the campaign.

Because she had a news background, Albright-Hanna focused on creating content that resonated with the campaign's audience. They leveraged a YouTube channel for connecting with the audience, and it became one of the most popular and effective tools of the campaign. The team produced over 1,500 videos and received over 20 million views on YouTube.

Hiring Lesson: Entertain vendor proposals to seek out talent.

Recruiting Campaign Talent—Develop a Pipeline

Bridgespan Group, a nonprofit management organization, suggests that nonprofit leaders, which political candidates are, look at building a talent pipeline to always have talent available.

In their guide, *Building a Talent Pipeline*, Bridgestar's Kathleen Yazbak suggests hiring with a people strategy. She recommends completing an informal needs assessment to determine what skills a nonprofit will need to support growth. This method applies to the political campaign as well.

Frances McLaughlin, chief operating officer at Education Pioneers, suggests thinking about the roles in your campaign organization in visionary terms—What do they look like "in terms of behaviors, mindsets, skills, and experience?"[6]

McLaughlin suggests selecting the "best person *for the role*." Determining what the campaign needs and how the potential team member affects the campaign in several areas defines how to strategically approach hiring decisions within your campaign.

Because new media teams are still relatively novel, it may be difficult to find talent that meets your strategic requirements. Yazbak suggests turning to your existing personal network—current and former employees or colleagues and volunteers for talent leads.

Building a Diverse Team

Looking at the Obama campaign team, diversity was a key to the success of their outreach. McLaughlin said that "the drive to have a talent pipeline filled with diverse candidates must come from the top of the organization." Yazbak suggests forging partnerships with organizations that support diversity in their membership. She referenced looking to organizations that offer leadership training programs as a good starting point.

Forge Relationships with Education Institutions

Sandra Sims, owner of the website CauseBlogger.com, said this is a great starting ground for recruiting talent to your campaign. She recommends recruiting college students or new graduates with backgrounds in business, political science, web design, public relations, communications, or marketing.

The Right Mix of People Spells Success

In summary, the political communications team changed dramatically as online strategies evolved in significant ways during elections from 2000 through 2010. This 10-year preamble, offering incremental online tactics, has set the stage for candidates to be able to rise quickly from obscurity to fame—and to fall from the public's eye—or good graces, just as fast.

Thus, today's political communications strategy starts with a talent revolution that bridges the tried-and-true methods of marketing with the new online communications tools. Finding the right mix of people to bring innovation, diversity and traditional campaign planning methodology to this strategy is the key to success.

---

1 Harfoush, R. (2009) *Yes We Did! An Inside Look at How Social Media Built the Obama Brand.* Berkeley, CA. 55-58

2 Harfoush, p. 17

3 Harfoush, p. 18

4 Harfoush, p. 19

5 Harfoush, p. 141

6 Bridgespan Group. *Building a Talent Pipeline. n.d. Web.* (2010, 12 September) http://www.bridgestar.org/Library/BuildingTalentPipeline.aspx

CHAPTER 4

Candidate 2.0—Create Your Candidate's Personal Brand

PERSONAL BRANDING is a game-changer for political campaigns. America's ambitious shifted the focus from self-improvement to packaging *strategically* what was already there. Given that politicians are certainly ambitious, pragmatic by nature, and won't last long if they don't have image and perception down cold, personal branding has become the perfect tool for this group.

After personal branding became embedded in the political consciousness, social media came along. It added an almost exponential reach. And politicians went for it. No surprise, as Clay Schossow of New Media Campaigns notes, "Social media offers the rare example of a marketing strategy on which politics isn't twenty years behind."[1]

By now, political candidates and incumbents who understand social media have been able to leverage it for test-marketing, connecting with local voters, enabling supporters to build their own grassroots campaigns including special events, providing the public service of getting out the vote, fundraising, having a message resonate regionally, nationally, and globally, seamlessly meshing online and offline activity, and initiating immediate course correction at the first sign of trouble.

But those who may not appreciate it well enough, as seemed to be the situation in 2008 with Hillary Clinton's presidential run, and in 2009 with Massachusetts Attorney General Martha Coakley's bid for U.S. Senate, wind up losing elections. The social media proposition, as applied to politics, is binary: candidates who use it well can increase the odds of winning; those who use it poorly can increase the odds of losing, often in a more globally publicized way. Hence, we will examine the intersection of politics, personal branding, and social media as the U.S. moves toward a new model of running effective campaigns. The ideal campaign will be one equipped to cherry-pick opportunities, avoid perils, and shift tactics with confidence and speed.

The roots of personal branding trace back to 1980. In their book *Positioning*, marketing experts Al Ries and Jack Trout hammered the importance of creating a unique identity designed to dominate the marketplace. Anything less would fade amidst the growing glut of people, products, and services. The actual term "personal branding," became mainstreamed in 1997.

That's when management consultant Tom Peters published his now iconic article, "The Brand Called You."[2] Since then, there have been myriad versions of that. For example, in 2005, consultants W. Chan Kim and Renee Mauborgne wrote *Blue Ocean Strategy* which reinforced the need to create fresh space in an overcrowded marketplace. This resonated with politicians. After all, so many campaigns are built on sweeping out the old, with a promise to bring in something new.

Time and again, the power of social media has been documented in case studies of the 2008 U.S. election campaign. But the digital technology, what is known about leveraging it, how it must be integrated with non-digital tactics, the political issues, and the national mood have mutated since that time and continue to do so.

To begin, there is now formal research, not just generalizations derived from tracking and perhaps making inaccurate cause-effect assumptions. One study by Vivaldi Partners confirms that social media is not a strict numbers game, as was mass marketing. Rather, its objective is to create a specific online presence that serves as a pull force. The Vivaldi research found, for instance, what mattered more than the raw number of followers on Facebook and Twitter was the *kind* of followers. Of greatest value were those who assumed the role of brand ambassador and advocate.[3]

In addition, there have been campaigns, such as the recent Massachusetts Senate race, which proved that leveraging social media requires those with expertise in that field. Hiring expensive political experts without that experience won't get you there. Moreover, yesterday's innovators or brand names might not cut it today amidst technology and issues that change at breakneck speed. Recruiting digital campaign help demands seeking out just-in-time talent. Brand-name "experts" made in the last campaign are increasingly turning out to be one-trick ponies amidst the current volatility. One nice side effect to this could be reduced costs when hiring relative unknowns.

The Social Media-Centered Candidate

Without doubt, social media applied to politics is a dramatically different game than other types of tactics for perception management. Moreover, the game can change on a dime. The classic instance of those new realities is the growing global interest in politics. Where business was in the 1990s as a topic of fascination, politics is now. The election in Britain or Brazil is of as much interest to those in China and the U.S. as any of their own local or national elections.

Because of the worldwide reach of social media, there is no longer that entity called "the local election" in the sense that all elections now have the potential for global reach. Candidates must factor in these diverse audiences into their communications. Another result of this additional reach is the expanded base for fundraising.

Importantly, the online presence and the face-to-face persona must mesh. Both are necessary. In fact, so much of fundraising is done to support those ads for television and travel to in-person appearances and editorial conferences with mainstream media.

This is a media-savvy era. Therefore, most publics are sophisticated enough to discern that each medium—print, digital, video, audio, and in-person—presents candidates in a different way. However, those ways can't undermine the messages coming from each. While it may seem tempting to version a candidate based on region or issue, this has become a rookie move that creates dissonance as constituencies become confused and often annoyed.

One example of such misalignment was Carly Fiorina's Demon Sheep online attack video. That could be a bad fit for her given her marketing background and position as one of the top global business leaders. Yes, the tactic got attention, going viral. But was that the right attention for that particular woman with that particular pedigree in that particular campaign? While the video was just one tactic and certainly not the make or break for an election win, Fiorina lost her attempt to unseat Barbara Boxer in the race for a seat in the U.S. Senate.

What follows are some of the fundamentals relevant to the use of social media for political personal branding. They have been derived from research, experience in the field, panel discussions, and the forecasts of futurologists:

Being fully there and defining "there" are always in flux. The "there" in the online space depends on the demographics of the targeted constituencies, how those segments consume their social media, in what mix, and during what hour. Currently, the long form (e.g., blogs) has less reach with those under 40. Even among the over-40 crowd, the preference is for shorter forms, such as tweets and texting. In all segments, social networks such as Facebook have increasing reach, including in surprise categories such as women between the ages of 55 and 65. Images and video speak louder than words, so Flickr and YouTube are must-have components. In 2009, Michael Bloomberg's campaign for a third term as mayor of New York, featured a diverse range of images and video. The campaign's 224,000 YouTube plays were equivalent to 448,000 30-second ads.[4]

What percentage of resources to invest in each depends on continual measurement and interpretation of the data, particularly with regard to new objectives. The bottom line is that the commitment to be fully there must be 100 percent and it must be sustained. Half-hearted efforts on Flickr will mark the campaign as not knowing what it is doing or, just as damaging, as desperate. A campaign never wants to be perceived as flailing about attempting to do everything. Those who stumble in this space open themselves to potential ridicule, so ensuring authenticity in tone, style, and image is vital. The apt analogy might be an older individual still flashing that photo from 20 years ago. In the new media space, this type of tactic just isn't going to work.

The reason for caution here is clear: negative impressions can be made by too much or too little of anything, and there is no room for candidates with a sense of entitlement. This is prime time and the players must be ready for it. Ironically that might include the appearance of being amateurish, that is, not too slick or overly institutionalized.

Typical mistakes include over-utilizing platforms such as Twitter, by tweeting every minute of the candidate's day. This comes across as push, not pull, and raises questions how the campaign managers are using their resources. Funding sources might balk at this use of time.

Best Practices for Positive ROC (Return on Candidate)

Campaigns must look for signs of success along the way, so that they can assess the return on their candidate's overall image. Every action a campaign takes is designed to produce what we will call a positive Return on Candidate (ROC). Some smart ways to achieve positive ROC include the following:

Having a distinct voice. Social media is a conversation. Way back in 2000, Doc Searls and his co-authors of *The Cluetrain Manifesto* noted that the Internet makes it possible and preferable for people to "communicate in language that is natural, open, honest, direct, funny and often shocking."[5] Unfortunately, until that advent of digital communications, the prevailing way of communicating was the stilted, spun, indirect, and disembodied language of corporations.

Even some gregarious, charismatic politicians have to shrug off that tradition of corporatese. A clear, distinct voice is the price of entry into political life. That might require a learning curve.

More and more, candidates are testing out their voices in low-risk ways. Those range from anonymous postings and commenting to delivering talks in low-stakes settings.

Of course, effective conversation demands a genuine understanding of the audience. Technology expert, Rob Enderle, notes that a political dialogue entails telling others what they want to hear just as they want to hear it in terms of tone, volume, pacing, word choice, and point of view. Former businesspeople, adds Enderle, have to learn to do this and usually don't. That's because they are in the habit of managing, not connecting.[6] In the 2010 midterms, both former business leaders, Fiorina and Meg Whitman, lost. But even political pros might have to prepare for a new kind of conversation which takes place on a global stage and one which will be closely deconstructed.

In addition, they might not be accustomed to taking and staying with a strong point of view. Actually that expectation is permeating most media, even *The Wall Street Journal*, which once hailed its coverage as "objective." Currently, online and offline, traditional forms of objectivity are often triggering boredom.

The challenge, of course, is that this online voice has to mesh with the offline voice, ranging from speeches to print articles in mainstream media. U.S. Secretary of State, Hillary Clinton has become adept at this. That might reflect her growing comfort with herself as herself. As a prerequisite, social media requires that politicians exorcise their demons before going digital.

Operating on a speedy metabolism. The web has established expectations of immediacy in communications, an immediacy that demands attention to quality. When an event develops, followers look for that rapid response, usually through a number of reach points, be they text message or on YouTube. This demands that a digital multimedia communications SWAT team be positioned to mobilize at a moment's notice. Excelling in this could turn out to be a tactic to own the territory on certain niche messages such as environmental or energy issues.

The web publication Politico.com gained influence and stole market share from the once-dominant *Washington Post* because it arrived on the scene with a rapid metabolism. Consequently, it became the first place to turn to for political breaking news, analysis, and the political grapevine. And it is also *the* space politicians want to be covered in.

The pitfall here is to overdo reporting, analysis, and commentary on developing events. This is sometimes known as the Online Wasteland or Wallpapering the Web with TMI (too much information).

Exploiting what doesn't pan out. Failing fast or falling forward has become the new and respected rite of passage. An ethos which sprung up in Silicon Valley where there has always been commercial volatility, the concept has now gone mainstream. *Wired* magazine published a special section on the correlation between a well-documented public misstep, followed by stunning success. One example provided was Bill Clinton, who learned plenty from losing an early election.[7]

To digital audiences, hearing about failure is compelling because they long ago rejected the happy-valley spin world of mainstream media. For some puzzling reason, old-line entities have been positioning crises from accidents in coal mines to oil spills, still in that controlled we-are-innocent way.

The most effective way of falling forward is through a mixture of online and offline presence, just as former John Edwards' aide, Andrew Young, has been doing it. His continual mea culpa has become his signature. Few may feel endeared to him, but his presence helped to bolster his goal advancing sales of his book.

One especially effective tactic is to piggyback on or actually arrange for third parties to create humor about the mistake. Sarah Palin's morphing into a pop-culture phenomenon has been helped by that.

Recognizing that the conversation is a two-way street. Being out there digitally means there will be response. Some of this reality can be managed by common sense. That's not new. Skilled politicians always choose their adversaries strategically. They anticipate the so-called negative impacts their words and actions will have. Union organizer Saul Alinsky grew this into a fine art. The problem comes when the backlash hasn't been expected or prepared for. However, this must always be a mandatory. After all, a number of politicians deliberately generate inflammatory material about their opponents with intent to stir up viral pushback.

VIVA LA TWEET?

French President Nicolas Sarkozy was the first to use email to bring the French into the controversial 2007 presidential debate, making him the first to use online political advertising.

French journalist Djamila Ould Khettab reports that five French journalists recently kept up with news via only Facebook and Twitter in an attempt to determine if micro-blogging service and social networking websites are reliable sources of information. Journalist Nour-Eddine Zidane was one of the participants in the experience and concluded that Facebook and Twitter aren't equivalent, in that with Twitter one can follow someone without being followed, contrary to Facebook.

"It's easier to keep up with news on Twitter than on Facebook, in that for most members Facebook is a hobby, not a way to keep updated," Zidane said. "I missed any important news during the experience, but some topics are not really developed, such as international, economic or political issues."

Because Twitter in France is not yet mainstreamed, the most popular topics are not necessarily relevant or representative of being newsworthy.

Peter Horrocks, BBC Global News Director, demanded that journalists become familiar with social media and use it more. He remarked that social media is not a fad and that journalists aren't doing their job properly if they don't use it.

Because Twitter arrived a bit later in France, many French have never heard of it and fewer than 1 million French have already joined it, according to IFOP. In 2009, France was ninth in country rankings of the most Twitter users, behind such countries as Germany, Australia, Canada and the UK, according to Sysomos, a social media analytics company.

Facebook is more popular, in that 15 million French, about 20 percent of global French population, are reported to have signed up.

"Micro-blogging can help to alert media about local news," Zidane said. "I don't understand why French media are so reluctant to use it as a new journalistic tool. This is not a threat for journalists."

It may not be a threat, but as of June 2011, it is now banned from French media programming, as the country determined it would no longer actively endorse Twitter or Facebook, two privately owned companies within its national media. So for now, the tweets from France may be few and far between, leaving journalists who had become accustomed to signing off with a request to fan or follow, feeling rather friendless. *Quel dommage!*

Khettab, Djamila Ould. "French media not yet fond of Twitter and Facebook." upiu.com. http://www.upiu.com/articles/french-media-not-yet-fond-of-twitter-and-facebook."

Brown, Devin. June 6, 2011. France bans Twitter/Facebook mentions http://www.cbsnews.com/8301-504943_162-20069431-10391715.html

Then there are those who might have assumed they had thought through their online tone and content, only to experience a nasty blow-up. Such could be the situation with Sarah Palin's use of Facebook as her space to pontificate. Among some of her subject matter back in 2010 had been support of Carly Fiornia in the GOP Senate primary. As Liz Goodwin reported for Yahoo News, Palin's strong base of Tea Party Express supporters rebelled. Quick on her Wall, Palin "updated her post to defend Fiorna's social conservatism. Her original post chiefly praised Fiorina's background as a businesswoman."[8]

Nasty pile-ons are common in the digital space. Their ability to go viral fast feeds their popularity. Among the tactics to manage attacks is having ready-to-go, third-party support—support that should always be arranged beforehand and before a crisis strikes. In addition, if a battle begins online, it must be fought online, at least initially. Likely it will migrate to mainstream media as well as in-person appearances. If they are skilled in search-engine optimization (SEO), the third parties can dominate the high-ranking positions on search engines.

Another is to treat the situation as serious. Therefore, the tone and content of response must have a certain degree of gravitas. But it can't use corporate-speak. And it can't refuse to participate or provide comment. Most importantly, since the situation is volatile, battle plans must maintain a degree of flexibility.

Also effective is to throw open the doors for advice and help from the general public. This invitation to co-create the solution could be the solution. Recommendations should be treated with respect. The best can be featured in the media, both online and mainstream, as has been the public's input on controlling the BP oil spill.

Simultaneously introduce and return to other topics. Nothing encourages attackers like observing that the prey is stuck in the trap.

In the 2012 campaign, social media itself is one of the top stories to cover. Politicians who want greater exposure will work their way into those stories. Not only will their own experience be sought, in addition, they can provide fresh material such as general polls, qualitative research, outside experts, and access to special briefings on social media. This is getting the edge by creating the perception of being the expert in a category, such as a geographic area, issue, or party affiliation. Soon enough, the time will come when such a knowledge base and experience level are commonplace in the field of impression management. Therefore, use it or lose it now.

---

1 Schossow, C. Using Social Media in Political Campaigns (Part 1). *New Media Campaigns*. n.d. Web. (2009, 24 September)
http://www.newmediacampaigns.com/page/using-social-media-in-political-campaigns,

2 Peters, T. The Brand Called You. *Fast Company*. (1997, 31 August) http://www.fastcompany.com/magazine/10/brandyou.html

3 Payter, B. Next Tech Five Steps to Social Currency. (2010, 1 May 1) http://www.fastcompany.com/magazine/145/next-tech-five-steps-to-social-currency.html

4 Lavoie, J. Bloomberg Campaign: Social Media Case Study. (2010, 3 February) http://www.josephlavoie.com/?p=225

5 Levine, R; Locke, C; Searls, D; Weinberger, D; McKee, J; Rangaswami, J.P; Gillmor, D; *The Cluetrain Manifesto*, Basic Books, (2000)

6 Enderle, R. Whitman and Fiorina: Why Tech CEOs Don't Have a Chance In Politics. *TechNewsWorld*, (2010, 12 April) http://www.techeworld.com/story/69733.html?wlc=1273436929

7 Lehrer, J. Accept Defeat: The Neuroscience of Screwing Up. *Wired*. (2009, 21 December) http://www.wired.com/magazine/2009/12/fail_accept_defeat/

8 Goodwin, L. Palin backs Fiorina, faces Tea Party Facebook backlash, *Yahoo News*. (2010, 7 May) http://news.yahoo.com/s/ynews/20100507/ts_ynews/ynews_ts1960

CHAPTER 5

What's the Message?

Your Content Strategy

A T ANY LEVEL OF POLITICS, the candidate's primary tool for motivating and persuading voters is the package of messages put forward by the campaign. Unless the candidate can win the voters' support by simply standing in front of a crowd or a TV camera, he or she is going to have to rely on both general and specific messages that will sway large enough numbers of voters to pull the correct lever or mark the correct box on the ballot.

Of course, such messaging doesn't all have to be calculated. In some cases, candidates feel passionately enough about issues that happen to resonate with sufficient voters, or are charismatic enough to attract sufficient voters, to win an election without crafting any message other than, "Here I am. This is me."

But most of the time, campaigns are successful because they develop winning message strategies and implement winning message tactics with few, if any, missteps.

Separate from outbound media including radio and TV, direct mail, and telephone scripts, the traditional vehicles for message development and dissemination include caucuses, fundraisers, townhall meetings, and a variety of campaign rallies. At each stop, the candidate offers the latest package of campaign messages and gauges their impact on the crowd. Later, backroom experts parse the crowd's apparent responses and, backed up by focus groups and expert survey analysis, offer suggestions for fine tuning the campaign's messages.

Today's social media, however, offers entirely new ways for campaigns to develop, test, and fine-tune their messages.

One obvious avenue for putting forth a modern campaign's messages is via a web-log, or blog. Candidates can blog every day on particular issues. In addition, the candidate or representatives of the campaign can scour the digital space for blogs and postings that cover relevant issues, and respond to these. As a matter of transparency, campaign workers should make clear they are posting on behalf of the campaign, and should never pretend their posts are coming from the candidate, personally. To build outreach, responses to other blogs and posts should include links to the campaign's own blog, which should also be featured on the campaign's web pages.

Responses to the original blog and to the variety of other campaign posts provide a valuable data set from which campaign analysts can obtain reliable and relevant information about the issues that people (who have seen the blog entries) care about most, as well as clues regarding how much these people care about each one. By statistical methods, it is then possible to map these responses against the population of likely voters in the election district to gain a strong sense of what moves the community of likely voters.

The campaign's social media profile pages offer other useful avenues for developing and spreading campaign messages. Each of the social media networks presents different opportunities to share details about the candidate, including room to expound about specific positions or to link out to campaign web pages that offer details and discussions on matters likely to be important to voters in the district. Because different social media attracts different demographics, it is both possible and useful to vary campaign messages—without contradicting other messages—to better suit the people who will see them.

For example, Reddit attracts far more men than women, while Facebook, Twitter, MySpace, and Ning attract far more women than men. Seventy percent of the people using MySpace are younger than 45, while 77% of the people using LinkedIn are older than 34. Just 13 percent of those on MySpace have college or advanced degrees, but more than half of those on LinkedIn have college degrees. There are many other variables to be considered within the world of social media.

In fact, granular information is available regarding the people within each of the networks, as well as the people who live in the election district(s) that the campaign is trying to persuade. This allows campaigns to conduct highly sophisticated and complex targeting of messages in ways that simply were not cost-effective, or even possible, in the past.

Many campaigns have already discovered the power of social media to emulate traditional American Townhall meetings. In these highly personal and unpredictable venues, candidates are exposed to the raw thoughts and feelings of their constituents, and, in turn, are expected to expose themselves to voter scrutiny. Traveling the countryside to arrange and attend these townhalls can be time-consuming and expensive. How much more cost-effective and convenient it is to run virtual townhalls from the relative comfort of campaign offices, at the same time reaching more people and having access to resources, coaching, and tools that are likely to prevent the candidate from flaming out, melting down, or otherwise wrecking in the heat of real-time discussions.

Certainly, communicating online offers campaign representatives and the candidate multiple opportunities to avoid mistakes and provide measured responses to even the most provocative outpourings from constituents. But that isn't enough to guarantee success in campaign messaging.

It is vital that campaigns focus on presenting a package of messages that covers the full range of issues likely to be decisive in the upcoming election, a package that reflects a consistent set of positions and values, that is simple enough to be readily understood, and that resonates well with the candidate's base.

San Francisco's Mayor Plugs In

Two-term San Francisco Mayor Gavin Newsom likes Facebook and Twitter, not only for campaign purposes, but for present, everyday use. However, he favors YouTube. About once a week, he uses YouTube to speak to his constituencies on up-to-date issues. He clearly understands YouTube as a platform for "getting personal" with users. Newsom posted a video of himself signing legislation that promotes the social value of San Francisco and explains why it is important to him and his constituencies.

Brian Purchia, Newsom's former Deputy Communications Director, carries a hefty resume and was extremely instrumental in getting Newsom elected. Purchia first started working with Newsom in 2006 and was described by the *San Francisco Chronicle* as Newsom's "go-to guy for new and especially social media," and for implementing a groundbreaking new media strategy.

In 2009, Newsom met some of the city's leading technology entrepreneurs. Shortly afterward, city officials announced the launch of DataSF.org, a site for thousands of pieces of information pouring out of local government. DataSF.org makes available more than 100 data sets from local government, including public information from the police, the transport authority and public works.

Former Deputy Communications Director Purchia said that it made sense since it is the public's data.

Two months after DataSF.org was launched, the project reaped rewards from San Francisco's huge community of programmers. EveryBlock, a local data service, helped residents track calls to 311, the number used for requests to fix broken streetlights, potholes, blocked drains, and more.

Purchia said that the 311 tracker was proof of the value of openness.

"The use of Twitter and other online communications allowed citizens to send complaints and find information about city services," remarked Purchia. "Not only was information pumped out, but ideas and suggestions from citizens as to how to run the city were brought in."

"Using Social Media to Rally Support for Politicians"
http://www.articlesbase.com/marketing-articles/using-social-media-to-rally-support-for-politicians-2659841.html.
http://bayarea.blogs.nytimes.com/2010/02/19/gavin-newsom-the-twitter-prince/.
http://www.cnn.com/2009/TECH/12/28/government.web.apps/index.html.
http://www.guardian.co.uk/technology/2009/oct/14/san-francisco-open-city-data.

To accomplish this, campaigns are learning to use social media not only to disseminate information, but to hone the platform.

One change is that campaigning has started to become an iterative process. That is, the days of crafting the perfect message and sending it out to every voter are gone. Today, there is no one "right" message. Successful campaigns recognize that powerful messaging is an evolutionary process. A good message may quickly be undercut by an opponent, or by events, and require an immediate and possibly significant redrafting.

Social media also makes it possible for campaigns to elevate the whole conversation to a higher level of interest and engagement. Most people vote because they're concerned about one or more issues, and they vote for a particular candidate because they believe he or she has the best chance of getting things done in ways the voter will appreciate and approve of.

With social media, candidates can develop messaging strategies that support this view of politics by containing and conveying more substance, more two-way conversation, more listening and learning by the campaign, and a greater willingness to engage with voters on specific issues. Social media makes it possible for campaigns to shape policies in response to supporters' ideas and preferences.

For much of this work, messaging is now the best mechanism. Social media presents not just new messaging tools, but a chance to reset how we consider and approach campaigns.

However, as is true with any new paradigm, social media opens twin doors to both favorable and unfavorable events. For example, there is the new danger that holding back or refusing to evolve campaign messages can create a backlash among voters who, in years past, might have been willing to support such a stodgy campaign.

What's more, social media requires relinquishing a good measure of control. As a result, mistakes will happen, and external sources will be able to circulate unwanted messages within the base. Fortunately, the people who use social media tend to be as forgiving as they are demanding.

If you readily acknowledge your mistakes, if you learn from them, and if you reflect these responses onto the questioning and the comments that your actions provoke, most people will recognize these as signs of campaign development and will allow you to move forward from there. The key, of course, is not just disavowing errors, but reflecting indicating clearly you've heard what constituents are saying, and are willing to respond.

Fortunately, social media provides an exciting and wonderful opportunity to benefit from constituent experiences that are unanticipated and different. Campaigns are using social media to learn about and adapt to political realities within their groups of supporters. Instead of simply pushing out messages and testing constituent responses to them, campaigns are now able to develop and sustain a messaging process that creates an ongoing dialogue between the candidate and the voters.

With social media, it is no longer about controlling campaign messages. It's about directing and shaping campaign messages in response to what you have heard from the people with whom you are engaged.

What may be most exciting about social media is the inherent emphasis on sharing. People who like what they see and hear are prone to pass that information along to others in their personal social media networks. Online technology permits campaigns to offer several tools to facilitate this, such as a "forward to a friend" functionality, which makes it easier for campaigns to track who forwards messages, where, and when; and customized buttons that allow recipients to add a link to the campaign's message to their own postings on social networks such as Twitter, MySpace, Digg, and LinkedIn.

Since voters who like a candidate are likely to have friends who may be similarly inclined, social media provides a ready mechanism to spread the campaign's messages far and wide without a lot of extra effort.

Create Your Stump Speech

As social media becomes more popular and more mainstream, ever-increasing numbers of political candidates are turning to online tools to reach voters and volunteers, drum up support and even raise money for their campaigns.

Candidates have realized that people are no longer satisfied receiving information about candidates through static media such as newspapers, radio, and television. Social media allows them to access the information they want, when they want it.

Social media is perfect to help in political campaigns because there has never been an easier way to connect with countless numbers of supporters. In the past, candidates and their staffs have had to deal with time-consuming and impersonal tasks such as bulk mailings and automated phone calls to reach voters. With only a few keystrokes, social media can connect candidates with all of their supporters and prospective supporters. Social media lets candidates learn from and share their views with people they might never have met.

Social networking sites such as Facebook, Twitter, YouTube, Flickr, and blogs, as well as new twists on traditional campaign methods such as online townhall meetings make it easier for candidates to disseminate their messages. They can make announcements related to their campaigns, engage voters on pertinent issues, and organize events.

Not only that but these social media tools can also help candidates save time and money and reduce their workloads because they don't have to send out countless letters or other mailings, email constituents individually, or make fruitless telephone calls to the masses. Candidates can now afford to be more targeted with their one-on-one message strategy, reserving the most customized communications for those who are most engaged.

Candidates would also do well to repurpose content they've created for other purposes. Letters written to constituents regarding a candidate's stand on an issue could be used to provide content for a blog post.

Additionally, those seeking elected office can use social networking sites to post videos, news articles and press releases and to respond to questions and concerns from constituents. And these tools give candidates more control over their images and messages, allowing them to paint themselves in a positive light and to frame their messages in the ways they see fit.

Whatever way candidates chose to disseminate content, it is important that the content be meaningful to their campaigns in one way or another. Even posting the name of a favorite movie, book, or musical group can give people insights into the personality of a particular candidate.

The main point for candidates to remember is not to join social networking sites if they don't have the time or the resources to actively participate in them and update them frequently. There's nothing worse than a social networking site that lacks content because it gives people the impression that a candidate has nothing to say, and worse, that the candidate just doesn't care.

But no matter how candidates connect with people, they have to make sure there's also a way for those people to connect with them. For example, a page where constituents can sign up to volunteer on behalf of a campaign; a way for them to offer comments and suggestions; and, of course, a way for them to donate money.[1]

Because navigating the sheer numbers of online social media sites and social networking tools can be daunting at best and overwhelming at worst, it is better to focus on the more popular of these sites and tools.

Global Snapshot: Brazilians Big on the Microblog

Brazil ranks fifth in the world in terms of the population of Internet users and is a country that is well-versed in digital technology. Out of a population of 195 million, 72 million Brazilians have Internet access. In 2009, the number of mobile phones reached 176 million, and Brazil ranked second in the world of Twitter subscribers, with more than 10 million accounts.

Because the number of Brazilians who use new technologies is growing, presidential candidates for the October 3, 2010 presidential election focused on new media, including social network websites Facebook, blogs, Twitter, SMS and the popular Orkut.

At the time of the elections, presidential candidates Jose Serra, Brazilian Social-Democrat Party, had over 213,000 Twitter followers, Dilma Rousseff, Labour Party, had approximately 40,000 Twitter followers, and Marina Silva, Green Party, had close to 29,000 Twitter followers. Because Rousseff was well aware of the 2008 U.S. election success that stemmed from Twitter, YouTube, and other digital technology, she hired an American company to try to repeat this success in Brazil. Thus, a team was assembled, ready to post positive comments for her, as well as defend possible attacks in blogs and political websites.

The efforts seem to have paid off, for Rousseff won the election handily with 55 percent of the votes.

d'Essen, Caroline. "On the social media campaign trail in Brazil." rnw.nl/English/article.
",http://www.rnw.nl/english/article/social-media-campaign-trail-brazil.
http://riotimesonline.com/news/rio-politics/dilma-campaign-to-cost-r187mm/.
http://riotimesonline.com/news/rio-politics/dilma-campaign-to-cost-r187mm/.
http://adage.com/globalnews/article?article_id=139378.

Perhaps the best of the social networking sites for soliciting votes, volunteers, supporters and donations is Facebook, which allows candidates to post pictures, add videos, send detailed mass messages, publicly interact on walls, and more. Most candidates probably already had Facebook pages set up before they decided to enter the political fray. If not, it's a sure bet they created Facebook pages as part of their campaign strategies.[2]

While Facebook can be an important forum in a candidate's campaign toolbag, it is important to understand the difference between a personal Facebook page and a Facebook fan page.

People who have personal Facebook accounts have to approve each person who asks to be listed as a friend and who wants to interact with them online. For public figures looking to amass large groups of supporters, this strategy is simply not feasible or wise. Rather, political candidates should create a type of Facebook fan page called a politician page, and allow anyone to join or become a supporter.

It is not hard for candidates to create Facebook fan pages for their campaigns. They will simply need to build this page from an existing personal Facebook page. The administrators of the page have control over their supporters, their content, and how they promote their pages.

Candidates can use their politician pages to build up contact lists of supporters and keep those supporters informed about their campaigns. They can update their supporters on their activities with bulk messages or calls to action; allow them to post and interact on their politician page walls; and promote their political pages via other websites and online media.[3]

To create buzz about a politician fan page, the candidate should link this to his or her main campaign website. The candidate should also let all Facebook friends know about the politician page and ask these friends to sign on as supporters as well as to publicize the page to those on their email lists. A politician fan page makes it easy for candidates to communicate their messages to large numbers of people.[4]

Once a candidate sets up a politician fan page, he or she should ensure that an expert is placed in charge of this effort— ideally, someone who knows Facebook Markup Language and has marketing expertise. Ensure that the page administrator adds some graphics to the page including an eye-catching banner, photos, and videos.[5]

And a candidate should decide on a good name for the Facebook politician page because that name has an effect on search results.

When people search for a candidate on Google or Yahoo or Bing, it is important that the candidate's name be one of the first served up by the search engines so he or she won't be missed. Candidates can use Facebook ads to drive traffic to their Facebook pages by using the "social ads" configuration to connect their pages with their ads.[6]

Candidates should regularly monitor their pages for inappropriate or abusive comments and delete them. However, they should make sure to have a transparent and publicly-stated strategy for dealing with these comments. But candidates really shouldn't delete comments that might make them look bad because, most likely, their supporters will respond to those comments and begin a dialogue with each other.[7]

For political candidates who are frequently on the go and don't have as much time to sit down at their computers and post to Facebook, then Twitter might be a better social networking tool for them to use. Candidates can use tweets to update other Twitter users who have subscribed to their accounts on what they're currently doing.

While Twitter isn't as interactive as Facebook, candidates should set up a Twitter account and encourage supporters to subscribe to their tweets to receive updates about their campaigns. By linking their Twitter accounts to their Facebook accounts, candidates' tweets will automatically be posted on Facebook, so updating constituents is easier. Candidates should also link their Twitter accounts to their campaign websites. Candidates can connect to their blogs via TwitterFeed and they can employ help from campaign workers to reach out to their Twitter followers by asking engaging questions.[8]

Twitter's audience is growing rapidly. Its followers include bloggers, journalists and political activists—groups that can influence a candidate's campaign. And candidates who tweet regularly and have something of value to say, can expect their followings to grow.[9]

Another way to develop followers and supporters is to retweet or repost their content, giving them full credit, of course.

Online video is another way for candidates to reach supporters. Through free video-sharing websites such as YouTube, candidates can create their own channels where they can share inexpensive videos with supporters. They can also embed the videos on their own websites and other social networking sites.

YouTube has become a particularly useful way to connect with people. Often people will bypass Google in favor of YouTube to look for information, making it the second-most-popular search engine in the United States. To ensure that people find their content, candidates should title, tag, and explain each YouTube clip carefully before uploading it. Including a link back to their websites in the description of the clip is also a good idea, and when possible "watermark" clips with the site's URL so that it is visible as the piece plays.[10]

A video is a powerful way to tell a story or make a political point because people have stronger emotional reactions to it than they do to text or photographs. But candidates would do well to remember that an online video isn't television, so it is important that the content, whether a speech or campaign footage, be authentic, substantive and stimulating, rather than merely aesthetically pleasing. A two- or three-minute video introducing a candidate and highlighting the important parts of the campaign is a good idea because viewers won't usually watch a video that is much longer.[11]

Political candidates should film their own short campaign videos and not only upload them to YouTube and their own websites, but send links to promote their campaigns to supporters in an email. They should also send press releases announcing their YouTube channels to the media.

On YouTube, candidates can also see exactly how many times their videos have been viewed, allowing them to measure effectiveness during their campaigns. And even if just a few dozen voters tune in, that's still a good amount of local campaign attention for something that costs nothing to produce.[12]

It is also wise for candidates for political office to upload campaign photos to Flickr, an image- and video-hosting website, web-services suite, and online community. Candidates can use Flickr to acknowledge volunteers and use the site's geotagging functionality to promote themselves to the communities that they visit. Candidates can also use Flickr to produce the photo stream of pictures on the photo page of their campaign website. And candidates can link to their campaign websites from their Flickr accounts.[13]

Candidates with well-run Flickr accounts let supporters know that they are willing to pay attention to detail, so they should create great titles and descriptions about every photo they upload into their accounts.

The range of possibilities is almost endless when it comes to platforms. For example, Microsoft's TownHall, is a plug-and-play, web-based platform hosted on Windows Azure, Microsoft's cloud computing platform, which candidates can use to build websites to engage supporters in campaign issues and to encourage them to participate in the process.

Microsoft's TownHall can be used to collect feedback from supporters and gauge their interest regarding various topics. The platform helps candidates organize, moderate, and house online conversations, driving discussion around constituents' issues and concerns. People can join the conversation on any web-enabled device. With TownHall, candidates can include poll questions as well as let people ask and answer questions. The most popular or relevant questions bubble to the top, so candidates can see what people are talking about.

It's The Consistency, Stupid

Gone are the days of getting away with stating one position in a speech in Iowa and reversing that position in a California townhall. The media is quick to cite the discrepancies and call foul—and then tweet, post, and blog about it almost instantly. Even modifying one's speaking style based on audience, known as code-switching, while it may be politically savvy, is becoming more and more problematic as speeches can now be videotaped from across the globe and accessed in succession, thereby exposing the often dramatic changes in linguistic style.

For example, Christopher Beam notes that in the 2008 primaries, Hillary Clinton, John Edwards, and Barrack Obama were all faulted for their disingenuous and/or simply shoddy attempts at a Southern drawl, Southern "poor-mouthing" and "talking black" to black audiences, respectively.

That said, candidates must optimize the fact that they can time-shift their messaging and reach out to more diverse constituencies than ever before. They simply must do so with an eye toward consistency—forming just one authentic candidate for voters to see.

For instance, candidates can use online townhalls to allow voters to offer their opinions, prioritize issues, and offer insights into those issues. They can also set up an online suggestion box where voters can post ideas, and other members of the community can vote those ideas up or down.

Similarly, candidates can host teleconferences and online meetings to discuss their policies and other topics such as decriminalizing marijuana, which may not usually surface within a traditional press conference. The chances someone will vote for a particular candidate increases when that person has a chance to interact with a candidate and have his questions answered firsthand.[14]

Blogs can also be used by candidates to reach constituents. Campaign staffers can participate in a discussion via the comments sections of most blogs. Campaigns should look for blogs that focus on issues they care about, such as immigration, education, or gay marriage, hoping to pick up financial or other support from outside their immediate districts.

And candidates can deliver their messages by asking the authors of popular or relevant blogs if they might be willing to guest blog. Candidates should also consider advertising on political blogs because such ads are relatively inexpensive ways to reach voters.

Some political candidates have their own blogs on their campaign websites. The problem, though, is that most of them are not written by the candidates themselves. Rather, they're just news articles, videos, or other pieces written by campaign supporters or staffers.

Candidates who choose to have blogs should add different types of media to their blog posts. An example might be integrating videos from YouTube to better engage their readers. And candidates who allow people to post to their blogs may increase their support because those people feel more connected to their campaigns.

Although blogs can help candidates show more of their personalities than, say, a press release, blogs take up fair amount of time. Any candidate who launches a blog must be sure to constantly add content to keep people interested and to keep them coming back.

Depending on a candidate's message and who exactly the candidate wants to connect with, other social media sites can also be useful. For a candidate who has a strong background in business, LinkedIn is a good choice. And candidates who are looking to reach a younger, hipper group of people can find out where the hip hang out these days and start a conversation there.

To raise money, candidates can turn to the social media site, GoFundMe, where they can create online donation pages, share them with friends and family through email, Facebook, Twitter, and begin collecting money online. GoFundMe connects directly to candidates' PayPal accounts. And candidates can embed donation pages on their blogs or websites.

Using the GoFundMe dashboard, candidates can also track donations. Every time someone makes a donation, GoFundMe sends the candidate an email. After receiving the email, candidates can see the new donation appear in their GoFundMe dashboards and inside of their PayPal accounts.

GoFundMe awards grades to users based on how well they attract donors to their funds. Candidates can post "Updates" to share news about their funds with their supporters to help attract more donors. GoFundMe doesn't charge any transaction fees—only a monthly subscription of $9 for each donation page.

After leverging the mainstream social media networks, candidates should look to sites that focus on specific niches with which they have an affinity—veterans' sites, for example. In this way, candidates can capitalize on those connections.

But no matter what social media networks candidates focus their attention on, the most important fact to remember is to continually update their content and keep their sites current and aligned.

1 Delany, C. How Candidates Can Use the Internet to Win in 2010. Epolitics.com (2010, Feb. 2010) "http://www.epolitics.com/winning-in-2010.pdf"

2 Facebook Fan Pages for Political Candidates and Campaigns. *Killer Campaigning Political Campaign Strategies: How Candidates Run for Office & Win Local Elections* (2010, 4 January) "http://www.killercampaigning.com/facebook-fan-pages-for-political-candidates-and-campaigns/"

3 "Facebook Fan Pages for Political Candidates and Campaigns."

4 "Facebook Fan Pages for Political Candidates and Campaigns."

5 Goldfarb, S. Top 10 Strategies for Running a Facebook Political Campaign. *All Facebook* (2009, January)http://www.allfacebook.com/2009/01/top-10-strategies-for-running-a-facebook-political-campaign/

6 Goldfarb

7 Goldfarb.

8 Political Campaign Tweets: Twitter, Candidates & Elections. *Killer Campaigning Political Campaign Strategies: How Candidates Run for Office & Win Local Elections* (2010, 7 January) http://www.killercampaigning.com/political-campaign-tweets-twitter-candidates-elections/

9 Delany, C. Winning in 2010: Online Outreach. *techPresident* (2009, 6 October) "http://techpresident.com/blog-entry/winning-2010-online-outreach"

10 Delany, C. How Candidates Can Use the Internet to Win in 2010. Epolitics.com (2010, February) "http://www.epolitics.com/winning-in-2010.pdf"

11 YouTube Political Campaign Videos for Local Elections. *Killer Campaigning Political Campaign Strategies: How Candidates Run for Office & Win Local Elections* (2010, 23 January) "http://www.killercampaigning.com/youtube-political-campaign-videos-for-local-elections/"

12 "YouTube Political Campaign Videos for Local Elections."

13 Presidential Candidates by Flickr Use (2007, 5 September) "http://www.jdharper.com/politics/FlickrCandidates.html"

14 Terrell, S. Virtual Town Hall Meetings Deliver for Candidates. Blog Post. (2009, 30 October)

CHAPTER 6
Research Your Base

IN RECENT YEARS, the entire cultural landscape has undergone a sea change, due in part to the prevalence of the Internet and in particular, to the growth in popularity of what is termed social media.

Social media sites, which include Digg, Facebook, LinkedIn, MySpace, Ning, Reddit, StumbleUpon, Twitter, and many others, have accumulated an avalanche of adherents. In the U.S., more than 60 percent of adult Internet users have created profiles on one or more of these networks—and that is likely to increase further, following well-established trends in other developed countries.

These social media profiles typically include a great deal of demographic, geographic, and lifestyle information about the people behind them. Even better, these social media software systems allow savvy researchers to tease out a wide range of additional details about these people's preferences, behaviors, values, and attitudes. As a result, social media is gaining recognition as a cost-effective tool for researching the base of favorable voters, along with other likely voters who may significantly alter the outcome of an election.

Communities: When to Create, When to Join

In the past, campaign research generally relied on old-school approaches such as focus groups, and telephone methods, including random digit dialing (RDD) to assemble investigative groups that were representative of election districts, registered voters, and even likely voters. Today, social media offers several significant advantages over these tried-and-true methods. Those include much faster turnaround times for surveys, lower costs for each completed response, enhanced ability to provide more detailed information to which people can respond, and improved potential to eliminate interviewer bias.

Certainly, there are undeniable and significant differences between actual voters and groups of respondents found via social media. But they are well recognized, and according to popular research, it is possible to compensate for these differences when analyzing survey results. The bottom line is that campaigns can use social media effectively to expand and improve their research efforts.

Moreover, social media provides simple and easy methods for targeting voters, thus allowing campaigns to use resources more efficiently. The foundation for this, of course, is to know who is going to vote and, who among those voters constitutes the candidate's base. Turnout depends not only on the up-ballot races, the issues, and the emotional heat of the election, but also on voter demographics including age, income level, education, ethnicity, and religion.

While much dialogue has been put forward about whether candidates should seek to create a new social media community or are better served by joining an existing one, experts widely agree that generally it does not make sense to form your own community.

Except in presidential campaigns, it is better for candidates to go where the voters are, rather than to try to attract voters to a brand new community. Local candidates rarely have enough passionate supporters to do so effectively. This conclusion is as convenient as it is practical, because most candidates have already joined at least one social media community as part of their effort to engage with the issues and the people within the district.

As a member of one or more communities, the candidate (and his or her surrogates who work the social media on behalf of the candidate—always openly making clear it is the campaign, not the candidate, who is communicating) should be careful to approach each of the social networks in its own way.

For example, Twitter generally allows for better one-on-one conversations than Facebook, which is more oriented toward one-to-many interactive engagements.

Imagine, for example, that a city council candidate wants to tap into a natural support base of voters who care about environmental and educational issues. The candidate can easily search for people within each social media network and within the election district who are already talking about those issues, and can readily engage with them by responding to their posts, offering links to campaign position papers or policy statements, and answering questions or helping to suggest solutions to problems.

Campaigns can also establish their own social media pages within Facebook and other social media networks, and encourage constituents to visit there. Most social media users are readily attracted to such pages, expecting them to offer more about the candidate's positions and ideas, to allow posting of responses and reactions to the candidate's initiatives, and to provide a mechanism for them to request "constituent services" regarding their problems or opportunities.

Politicians can benefit greatly from attracting people on particular social media networks to follow them, fan them or "like" them (the terminology continues to evolve). Such mechanisms make it easy to let interested people know what the candidate is doing, where the campaign is going, and what supporters can do to help win the election.

Compared to email or text messaging, which push information into the phones or mailboxes of listed recipients, social media allows followers and fans to retain far more power over what information they will receive, and when they will receive it. This changes the psychology and the dynamic of the relationship, making people far more willing to provide information and feedback to a campaign, and far more receptive to its messages.

While it is a rare candidate who can benefit from the creation of a new social media community, nearly every candidate can benefit from recruiting a group of loyal supporters into a new kind of research base. These "closed communities" of people, who have agreed to make themselves available for in-depth interaction with campaign officials, provide a readily available and inexpensive source of explanations, analyses, emotional reactions, and even new ideas, which the savvy candidate can incorporate into campaign strategies and tactics.

Within these closed communities, campaigns can float new ideas, solutions to problems, slogans and various spins on salient matters. The closed community's responses can reveal what larger groups of supporters may think and feel about these issues.

One goal of campaign research is to identify the issues most likely to motivate people to offer support and to vote favorably. These generally turn out to be the issues about which voters feel most strongly. Via social media, it is easier and less expensive than ever before to find clusters of people who are passionate about particular issues, and then to investigate their responses to campaign initiatives to identify which issues will prove most fruitful within the election district.

Another thread of campaign research is to identify biographical elements that will make the candidate most appealing to voters in the election district, and to downplay those who generate negative responses. Local candidates may already have favorable reputations and a great many individual relationships. Candidates in larger districts may need to rely on less-obvious factors. Each likely item— from ethnicity to track record—can be floated within the candidate's closed social media communities. Those that engender the most passionate support can be incorporated into the candidate's more general campaign.

Because so much is known about individual users of social media, it also becomes possible to look at cross tabulations that identify voters as members of particular groups, based on such factors as party registration, age, gender, location of residence, interests, ethnicity, education, and income levels. It is generally true that different groups will respond more favorably to different aspects of the campaign. Identifying these areas of resonance for each group of likely voters will help the campaign to allocate resources more effectively, maximizing the number of voters who receive messages they find appealing from the campaign, and (with luck) minimizing the number of voters who receive campaign messages that will turn them off.

DC Mayoral Race

In the Washington, DC mayoral race, the two main contenders, present Democrat Mayor Andrian Fenty, and Democratic candidate Vincent Gray battled it out with social media strategies.

Mayor Fenty's "Green Team" has had a Facebook page for some time, but the campaign focus, as in the 2006, has been door-to-door canvassing and rush-hour sign-waving more than tweeting and blogging.

Candidate Vincent Gray, who ultimately won the election over incumbent, Fenty. utilized Twitter, a campaign blog, YouTube, Facebook and more. Though Fenty had an established online presence, in June 2010, Fenty's Facebook page earned 996 "likes," but Gray quickly caught up with 949 "likes" on his newly established page. Thus is the power of social media.

"The idea is to run the most engaged online campaign that the District has seen," said Ian Koski, Gray's media director.

Fenty, concerned by Gray's social media tactics, upgraded his tech program and launched an upgraded Web presence, which included Twitter and a campaign blog, though he was slow to actively engage.

Social media can work both ways, in that if a candidate does something of which voters disapprove, word spreads quickly. For instance, Gray moved to cut funding on a particular streetcar run and pro-streetcar activists, via Twitter and the blogosphere, went wild. Gray saw his mistake and reversed the decision.

Fenty lost the opportunity to gain some votes from disgruntled people.

Koski calls the streetcar blowup "a good case study" for the power of social media. "People spoke up. They had an issue. The campaign knew about it, we saw it, and we did our best to engage," he says. "That's the power of the Internet."

DeBonis, Mike. June 2, 2010. "Gray outguns Fenty in the social media battle" voices. washingtonpost.com.
http://voices.washingtonpost.com/debonis/2010/06/gray_outguns_fenty_in_the_soci.html.

For example, the candidate's position favoring new street lighting may be greatly appreciated by neighbors who like the idea in general, but may be strongly disapproved by those who like the rural feel of their unlighted neighborhood, as well as by those who fear higher taxes to pay for the new lights. The same forces make it far more common for couples with young children to favor bond issues intended to support better schools, compared with senior citizens whose children are beyond school years, and who are therefore more focused on other issues.

The more granularly a campaign can analyze voters in an election district, the more accurately it can tailor its positions, policies, and messages. Traditional polling and research tends to deal with relatively small samples, limiting the validity and accuracy of any possible conclusions. Social media, however, allows for investigation of much larger samples without the heavy costs of traditional polling, and also raises the possibility of interacting directly with large numbers of voters.

One-on-One Engagement

Most pollsters highly prize what they call "verbatim responses," which are actual ideas and arguments put forward by survey respondents. In traditional media, they are generally not encouraged, may not be accurately recorded, and generally form a relatively small portion of the data flowing from the research back to the campaign. With social media, however, these "verbatim responses" are the meat and potatoes of the research, typed directly into the system by the voters themselves.

These responses can provide complete, nuanced, and wide-ranging snapshots of the exact phrases, the mindsets, and even the hot-buttons that are likely to drive voters' choices in the upcoming election. As such, they can provide a uniquely valuable source of material that campaign researchers can mine for insights into the most promising paths to victory.

In a 2009 issue of *Marketing Week*, Morag Cuddeford-Jones pointed out, "The emergence of social media has benefitted traditional research methodology by forcing it to become more engaging and interactive."[1]

For years, research pertaining to political campaigns has revolved around traditional approaches including historical comparisons, quantitative methods involving evaluations and surveys, and qualitative methods using ethnography. As social media continues to revolutionize advertising and marketing research for general business, it is also redefining standard research methods for political campaigns.

Social media allows unprecedented access to a candidate's constituencies, offering campaign organizers and analysts a new dimension in campaign research. As more and more people join and engage in social media sites, using relevant tools available through various public social networks, creating private social networking sites, and implementing social media monitoring services will become integral to optimizing any campaign research platform and actuating real results.

While social networks provide valuable quantitative research methods through various survey and polling applications, tapping into public social networks can also provide a useful alternative to traditional, qualitative research employing ethnography. Ethnography uses conversation, in-depth interviewing techniques and observation to learn more about people, as well as their influences and perceptions. Social media allows direct access to conversations and comments from willing participants, enabling a whole new dimension in qualitative research.

Of course, to take full advantage of the qualitative and quantitative research benefits available through social media, it is important that candidates be engaged with others involved in the online communities they are hoping to gain insight from. In a *PR Week* article stating, "Twitter, LinkedIn and Facebook communities can be effective ways to distribute opinion surveys targeting specific groups—particularly for new business and initial research phase," Eva Keiser, Senior Vice President at Risdall McKinney PR is quick to add, "Before you blanket social media sites with surveys, establish yourself within the community."[2]

Any candidate at any level in a political career should be actively participating in all of the four major social networking sites: Facebook, Twitter, LinkedIn, and YouTube. However, the campaign researchers should also be using these networks to compile information on voters to more accurately manage the campaign and to make adjustments as needed. David Erickson of Minneapolis-based Tunheim Partners public relations agency explained, "Candidates who study the ins and outs of Facebook and LinkedIn will come to realize the retail-politicking power of these tools. The sophistication of Facebook's new filtering tools will allow them to target very focused messages to very narrowly defined audiences."[3]

Facebook pages have become imperative for businesses and organizations, as well as politicians. Not only do they facilitate an open forum for communication among brands and consumers, as well as politicians and their constituents, but they also help to gather fundamental information that market researchers and campaign analysts would otherwise spend hours trying to accumulate. Facebook Pages can be created to represent a company or public figure, allowing individuals to show their support by clicking "like."

This will add the page to the supporter's personal profile and allow that individual to interact and engage with others on the page.

The Facebook Page also provides incomparable demographic statistics about supporters of the page through the "Insights" tool, which analyzes the demographic data, with regard to age and gender, of everyone who supports the page. When compared to average Facebook user statistics, researchers can use the information to determine which gender and age groups their campaign has not yet connected with. The data can be viewed in graph form or exported into an Excel file.

Facebook polls are another fast and easy way to ascertain research data through the social networking site. They can be created through the Facebook polling application and added to personal profiles or public pages. You will simply create the question and a set of answers, and share the poll with supporters on your candidate's page. The application handles all of the calculations, tabulating the results instantly. Polls can be used to gauge opinions on policies, how supporters are feeling about a candidate, or any other opinion-based questions.

Going through Facebook's ad-creation program will also give you instant access to core demographic information. You don't actually have to pay for an ad to benefit from Facebook's statistical information. Simply go to create an ad and enter anything in the URL box or, if you have a Facebook Page, click on the option pertaining to advertising something on Facebook. This will take you to the next step where you can choose specific demographic information, narrowing the results down by gender, age, education and interests. A floating box will appear in the right hand column with the total number of people who match your required demographic parameters.

Twitter has introduced another new frontier in social media research. Various applications are being developed constantly to improve methods for searching and locating information on Twitter. Twitter's search engine alone allows a real-time account of what is being said about any keyword that you enter. More importantly, Twitter can prove useful in collecting information on the opponent, as well as the opponent's constituents. Locating the opponent's followers on Twitter will enable you to gather data from their profiles and also keep abreast of what they might be saying about you. This can be helpful in pinpointing confusion that some may have regarding a candidate's views and goals.

Social in Massachusetts

Massachusetts Democratic Gov. Deval Patrick and his challengers Republican Charlie Baker, Independent Tim Cahill, and Green-Rainbow Jill Stein pulled out all the stops on social media in the November 2010 election campaign.

Most voters find it more fun and engaging to follow the campaign through blogs, Facebook, Twitter, and YouTube by participating in a dialogue with the campaign and its candidate. Politicians are finding that social media is an inexpensive way to reinforce their political messaging directly to their constituents, free of media bias.

Social media is a powerful campaign tool, in that candidates can bypass or supplement traditional media and send their message directly to supporters and potential supporters. It is also a way to build large databases of voters.

Juli Sweeney, Candidate Tim Cahill's press secretary, said that Cahill had a tremendous response when he used social media to promote his first supporter rally in May 2010.

"We asked people to donate $20.10 and tell 10 friends about the rally, using Facebook and Twitter," Sweeney said. "All donations were accepted online, and we ended up raising more than $20,000!"

Sweeny believes that social media allows people all across the state to hear Cahill—even if he's not able to meet with them face-to-face.

"It has helped supporters be involved in the campaign without having to physically be at events or in headquarters," she said. "And, as Tim looks to get more hands-on with our social media efforts, he hopes to be able to connect with people on a personal level—they won't need to turn on a TV or open a newspaper to get to know him."

Leccese, Mark. June 27, 2010. "Do you like me? Will you follow me? Social media in Mass. Gov. Race. http://boston.com/community/blogs/gatekeeper/2010/06/mass_gov_ candidates_wage_socia.html.
http://bostinnovation.com/2010/06/27/follow-the-massachusetts-governor%E2%80%99s-race-on-social-media/.
http://bostinnovation.com/2010/07/09/candidates-social-media-tim-cahill/

Similar to Facebook, several applications that enable Twitter users to survey their followers have been developed. The most popular of these is Twtpoll at http://twtpoll.com. This site allows Twitter users to create basic polls at no cost. There is a charge for creating more complex surveys, as well as collecting demographic information from participants, but the time saved is well worth the expense. Using social media as a means to conduct surveys and polls is quickly replacing conventional methods that were limited to mail-in responses and telephone surveys.

With Twitter posts limited to 140 characters, it is primarily used by candidates to provide short answers to questions or as a method for driving traffic back to the website where supporters will find more comprehensive content and other information about the campaign. Studying these click-through rates, using Google Analytics, and comparing them to a candidate's total number of followers may help determine the fundraising potential behind Twitter. According to a report from Nationaljournal.com, "While no official statistics are available, early data suggest the click-through rate (on Twitter) is in the mid-single digits, delivering much better results than email and other kinds of online advertising."[4]

The professional social networking site LinkedIn also offers tools that could be beneficial to campaign researchers. The LinkedIn Answers feature can be used to post questions within different targeted professional groups. For instance, on September 17, 2007, prior to the November 2008 presidential election, then Senator Barack Obama posted this question in the Small Business category: "How can the next president help small business and entrepreneurs thrive?"[5] He received more than 1,400 unique responses from the small business community. This type of research provides unparalleled advantages in formulating campaign efforts that target the needs of specific professional communities, as well as discovering potential financial contributors.

YouTube can be used to deliver messages to supporters by featuring campaign ads, interviews and online debates. Viewer comments can provide a wealth of additional, qualitative data, providing researchers with a gauge of how their candidate's public persona and presentation ability is being perceived. The instant feedback also enables campaigns to react quickly to any misperceptions that viewers may have formed.

Specialized Communities, Grassroots Effects

There are also public social networks geared toward specific ethnic groups. MiGente is the largest social network specifically aimed at Hispanic Americans while BlackPlanet touts itself as the largest Black community online and AsianAve is a community connecting Asian Americans. Utilizing these networks, as well as other networks targeting specific groups such as Glee, a community site for gays, lesbians, and everyone else, can provide valuable insight into these niche communities.

While public social networks continue to dominate online activities, many companies are turning to private or white label social networks to grow their brand and engage with a more definitive target audience. Private social networks offer complete control and flexibility to the creator, which can translate into unlimited research potential, particularly for campaign research.

Many of the platforms used to create private social networks offer the same functions and features of popular public networks, including user profiles, instant messaging, and much more. Private networks allow total control of who can join, thereby enabling the creation of social sites to specifically targeted communities.

Creating sites that provide unique social experiences is the key to attracting members and keeping them there. Knowing more about some of the most popular companies available for creating social networking sites will help you decide which one is the most suitable for your campaign research needs.

Ning is one of the most widely used services providing private social networks, offering a user-friendly creation process and an abundance of feature options. The service offers custom design options and member profile pages. With Ning, you are able to choose to make your community public or private, approve members before they can join, and moderate all photos, videos, chats, discussions, and events before they are posted. Ning also allows you to create groups within your social network.

A report from the Emerging Media Research Council cited Scott Brown's win over democratic nominee Martha Coakley in the Massachusetts 2010 Senate Special Election as a victory for social media as well, due largely to Brown's aggressive social media efforts. Brown's social media campaign included a private network, called Brown's Brigade, which was set up through the Ning platform. At the time of the January 2010 report, Brown's Brigade had 6,000 member supporters of Scott Brown. The report also says, "The level of customization makes Ning an attractive choice for campaigns that want to develop an individual presence outside the bounds of Facebook."[6]

The 2010 Iowa Governor's race between incumbent Chet Culver and Terry Branstad has led both of them to invest in creating their own private social networking sites. Like Brown, both contenders chose the Ning platform. Branstad's communications director, Tim Albrecht cautioned that it is difficult to forecast a return on these investments, saying, "That's what's so great about social networking and pioneering online efforts. It is in the hands of the campaigns and the supporters behind them. Where this goes next is anyone's guess."[7]

Shoutem is another popular design platform that allows users to create private mobile networks that can be location based or aimed at specific groups. As with Ning, Shoutem networks can be made public or kept private and they also offer a multitude of customization options. Companies using Shoutem include WE Harlem, Ranch and Rodeo and NFL Shouts.

NFL Shouts founder Hussein Yahfoufi explains his decision to create a private network saying, "We decided we wanted to have a Twitter-like site but just for the NFL community. I really like Shoutem because it has given us everything we needed to build our site without needing to do our own development. The mobile function is important to use. We've seen that the most traffic on NFL Shouts is during football games, so people can connect with each other at the ground."[8]

SocialGo allows the creation of private social networking with many of the same options available through Ning and Shoutem. Personal profiles, blogs, forums, and messaging tools are available. Multiple monetization tools are also available, allowing you to charge membership fees, host advertisements, sell products, and display classified listings.

The targeted access available through private social networks will offer researchers the same qualitative insights gained through ethnographic methods on large public networks, only the information will be collected from a more controlled and definitive group of people.

Social media monitoring services are another useful tool for collecting quantitative campaign research. An array of services is available for anyone to research and record what is being said at any given moment about any given topic. They provide an advantageous way to find out what others are saying about a candidate's opponent as well. More importantly, many of these services are available at little to no cost. There are many monitoring services to choose from and it is a good idea to incorporate several methods in your research platform to compare results for more accurate conclusions.

The Google Alerts monitoring service is easy, fast and free, however its reach is somewhat limited compared to other services. To use Google Alerts, all you need to do is enter the keyword search term that you want to track and an email address where you want the information sent. Google Alerts will then send you a daily email with a list of where your keyword appeared on the web by searching across the web including news and blogs.

Similar tracking is available for mobile, so if you plan on conducting a great deal of activity via the mobile stream (e.g., anything from SMS messaging, to Quick Response (QR) codes, to smartphone web data and mobile apps, try Google's free analytics solutions that are specific to mobile. Other mobile analytics vendors exist and offer varying degrees of custom analytics. These include Flurry, Bango, and PercentMobile, just to name a few.

SocialMention.com is another free monitoring service that works similarly to Google Alerts, except that it gives instant results of your keyword search rather than a daily email. It also analyzes the data, detailing everywhere the keyword was mentioned, how often on average it was mentioned and the quality of each mention. More importantly for political campaigns, this tool also rates the sentiment behind each mention of the word you select, meaning it will tell you how many mentions ere positive, neutral and negative.

This can be a fast and efficient way to assess how a candidate and the opponent are ranking among Internet users. Although, an April 2010 article from *PR Week* warns against placing too much weight on the sentiment measuring tools offered by social media monitoring services, saying, "Politics, like many topics, will be discussed with a huge degree of nuance, subtlety and sarcasm, so there is no substitute for real-life consultants who can expertly analyze the tone and implications of a comment and be in a position to act immediately if required."[9]

Larger corporations and larger political campaigns may want to spring for monthly fees associated with one of several more precise and advanced monitoring services. Services such as Trackur, Radian6 (clients include Pepsi, Microsoft and Kodak) and Scout Labs (clients include Coca-Cola, Disney and McDonalds) offer more comprehensive tracking and analysis while also providing detailed information in dashboard-type formats. One of the most significant differences with the paid services versus the free services is that they will also rate the influential power of the site where your candidate's name is mentioned.

Based on the research amassed to date, it is reasonable to suggest that while the platforms and uses may continue to morph and evolve, social media has become a permanent part of our lives with more and more users joining and participating in some form of social media each day. As social networking audiences continue to expand it becomes increasingly necessary for politicians to participate in social networks in order to reach a wider and more engaged community. The interactions, conversations and general willingness to take part in online activities present research potential that, while still in its early stages, should be regarded as a value-add.

It is also important to remember that social media should not be the only factor in a political campaign. Following the 2008 presidential election, the Europe Intelligence Wire released a study that concluded, "Future campaigns need to hire marketing people who are both strategic and tech-savvy and campaigns will have to be willing to…experiment with new tools, while continuing to use traditional tools like shaking hands and kissing babies."[10] A research plan that integrates social media research methods with more traditional approaches will give any campaign its best opportunity for victory.

1 Cuddeford-Jones, M. Market Research: Social media breathes new life into research. *Marketing Week*; (2009, 7 May) p25

2 PR Toolbox: Importance of SEO, utilizing social media research, more; *PR Week (US)*; (2009, 6 April) p21

3 Ojeda-Zapata, J.Politicians find a friend in Facebook: As Coleman showed, social media offer a direct line to voters; *The America's Intelligence Wire*; (2010, 24 January)

4 Herbert, D. Will Twitter Add a New Wrinkle to Campaign Fundraising?; *Nationaljournal.com*; (2009, 7 April)

5 http://www.linkedin.com/answers/startups-small-businesses/small-business/STR_SMB/95900-11932467

6 Social Media Use in the Massachusetts's 2010 Senate Special Election; *Emerging Media Research Council*; Proprietary Member Briefing; (2010 19 January)

7 WE THE PEOPLE: Finding new ways to engage constituents; *Gazette* (Cedar Rapids, IA) (2010 19, March)

8 Shoutem makes it easy for users to create private social networks; *Total Telecom Online*; (2010, 3 March)

9 Social media monitoring: Measurement—the experts at work; *PR Week (UK)*; (2010, 2 April)

10 Assessing BlackBerry Politics: Expert Who Tracked Presidential Candidate's Use of Social Media Says Political Potential Barely Tapped; *Europe Intelligence Wire*; (2009, 2 February)

CHAPTER 7

Research Your Opponents

MORE CANDIDATES ARE USING social media to communicate their messages to supporters. With tweets, blogs, text messages, Facebook wall posts, LinkedIn updates and more, social media channels are also an integral part of a political candidate's competitive strategy. From exploring other candidates to competing issues to determining responses and positioning statements, this chapter will give candidates the upper hand in terms of understanding competitors.

Exploring Other Candidates

Not all opposing social media is created equal. Researching other candidates via social media channels depends on how the opponent is using their channels. If the candidate lacks interaction with his supporters, it is not necessary to track the social media component. Using a simple RSS feed or website change monitoring utility can help you to stay abreast of website updates.

Following other candidates via social media could be useful if opponents are engaging supporters because this provides a window into how they interact, handle questions, handle controversy, and more. This is becoming easier and easier to find as candidates engage more and more within social networks.

The Benefits of Following Your Opponents

Following the social media accounts of opponents gives a candidate three key benefits: a feel for what tactics are more favored by a campaign, where the opponent is concentrating efforts, and other important campaign information. Candidates must be cautious in engaging in these campaign conversations because most operatives protect their accounts. Placing a few "key operatives" in the social space to pick up informative chatter will help a campaign increase awareness of the competition.

Strategic Tip—Link to Your Competitors
HubSpot—a company that specializes in inbound marketing—discussed the benefits of linking to competitors in a recent blog post. One key recommendation was to write responses to competitors' blog articles without "simply arguing with their point of view."[1] The benefit is that candidates who take this approach will show they are thinking of the voters and their best interests. And, by moving beyond the simple counterpoint and into the realm of value, the candidate builds credibility.

Get Information Before It Goes Public
Using social media to conduct research on opponents can have dramatic effects. Even in small towns that are just getting started in

the social media space, we see more and more in the way of online forums and activities. Sometimes candidates will create forums for the primary purpose of staging attacks against opponents, so you will want to ensure you are tuned in to these types of sites from to be able to address any content that is false or designed to disparage your client.

By watching online hubs of activity closely, you can garner the issues your opponents consider important. Through monitoring your opponents' sites, you can often access links to opponents' unpublished campaign materials. These materials can be helpful to your candidate in preparing for debates, positioning distinction on an issue, and more.

Candidates can gain intelligence and tailor messaging based on opponent's activities. For example, one local campaign posted a preview of campaign yard signs on Facebook a month before actually printing and placing these signs. This gave the opposing campaign plenty of time to create a response, which it implemented moments after the opponent's sign went public.

These types of insights can undermine or neutralize the opposing campaign and give your campaign an additional window of time in which to shape a response or a counter move.

Tracking Conversations to Predict Outcomes

Alterian, a customer-engagement technology company, analyzed social media conversations to predict winners in 16 key senatorial elections this year. By analyzing the volume of online conversations, share of voice per candidate, and consumer sentiment, the company predicted election winners based on their favorability ratings in the social space for seven elections. The favorability rating was calculated by combining positive and neutral social media mentions of each candidate and then dividing that number by a candidate's total number of mentions across social media platforms.

Social media favorability only failed to predict the election winner in Texas with the 2010 governor's race, where Rick Perry defeated Bill White. While Perry led in the percentage of conversations, his 16 percent margin (in conversations) was mostly negative commentary, according to Alterian.

The bottom line of tracking conversations? According to David Elridge, CEO of Alterian, "social media proved to be a strong indicator of an important milestone in American politics—something typically tracked through mathematical studies or research polls."

He continues, "Monitoring and analyzing conversations provides valuable insight, enabling organizations to make predictions for future behavior such as we were able to for this election."[2]

Learn the Opponent's Story

It is not enough to know an opponent's stance on an issue to be competitive in today's elections. Candidates must learn the story behind why a political leader embraces a policy or position. According to Stanchak, the real human experiences that candidates portray are the real key to gaining attention in the social space. Look for the story.

Stanchak quotes Jake Ward, vice president of the David All Group, an online communications firm, as saying that the best politicians are good at "telling stories about others as a way of explaining the importance of their policies." A key historic figure to study is President Ronald Reagan. Ward notes, "Rather than just making it about themselves and their ideas, great politicians can turn the script around and make the campaign about the voters."[3]

Your Listening Infrastructure

A social media listening infrastructure can be relatively simple or highly complex. Depending on the type of election, level of competition and need for information, a political team can dedicate a person or even an entire team to researching and monitoring the competition via social media. Many companies offer applications to help candidates conduct such research, but it is possible to conduct the research in house. The next few pages will highlight several key social media platforms and how they will fit into a listening infrastructure.

In order to listen to opponents, a candidate must first seek out where he or she has information on the Web. There is a difference in listening in real-time and conducting competitive research. The listening is the most important during a campaign, but the competitive research is vital before and during the campaign. To see how these two key elements work together, the next few pages will provide competitive research tips in addition to listening techniques.

Develop the Infrastructure to Listen

Ward (in Stanchak) notes that politicians "need to listen more," adding there is a voter expectation that politicians will create "the infrastructure to listen."[4]

How does this apply to candidates running for office? It starts with setting up channels to listen to supporters early on. However, in this chapter the focus is on researching opponents and issues to create a competitive edge for the campaign.

By developing an infrastructure to listen to opponents, a candidate can learn from opponents' triumphs and mistakes. Taking the high road is much easier when the candidate is informed in how the opposing team listens to its supporters. If an opponent struggles with listening to his or her base, social media listening will reveal the upset of the base, therein creating an opportunity for candidates to respond proactively with proof points or stories centered on how they solved for that voter concern.

LinkedIn

This professional networking site is more than just a place to display a resume or professional qualifications. It is a treasure trove of information on 80 million professionals, and it should be the first stop in competitive research of opponents.

What a LinkedIn Profile Reveals
- **Past work history**—Important information for making connections to potential supporters and/or agendas.
- **Depth and reach of business network**—If an opponent has an extensive network on LinkedIn, it is possible to make connections among causes, supporters, business interests and even where a candidate stands on issues. By cross-referencing comments on Twitter and LinkedIn

network activity, it is possible to gain deep insights on a candidate.

- **Presentations they may have authored and added to LinkedIn via SlideShare**—Find more support for issue stance in past business or political presentations.
- **Tweets that they may have added pertaining to their LinkedIn status**—Here, too, connecting tweets and LinkedIn activity can reveal important business dealings and information on a candidate's past activities and stance on issues.
- **Personal blogs they may host and commonly link to from LinkedIn**—Find out which supporters read the blog, gain insights on an opponent's personal opinions and topics, and learn what issues matter most to the opponent.
- **The amount of time they spent at every previous job**—This must be cross-referenced with other sources, but if an opponent is claiming expertise in a particular area, LinkedIn can help derive whether that experience is extensive or light.
- **How they present themselves on their profile**—The LinkedIn profile is a way for individuals to present themselves in a personal, professional ad. How candidates present their experience and qualifications can reveal much about how they will sell themselves to voters.
- **Recommendations—opinions of their work and character from previous colleagues, managers, subordinates, or friends**—LinkedIn recommendations can take two tones—superfluous or genuine. The people who give the candidate recommendations are yet another source for competitive intelligence. Read their profiles

and recommendations to understand more about those with whom the candidate associates.

Twitter—Make Connections Over Time

Since Twitter happened on the social scene, it has become *the* publicity tool for individuals, organizations, and campaigns. While not as prevalent in smaller markets, Twitter is a powerful competitive intelligence tool when comparing tweets over time.

Because Twitter is real-time, it is difficult to capture data through Twitter's basic search. It will only track information over the past 24 hours. There are several strategies to consider in tracking opponent activity on Twitter.

Use a Twitter tool to monitor tweets, followers, Twitter lists, and hashtags on issues and candidate names. The leading Twitter tools are HootSuite (www.hootsuite.com) and TweetDeck (www.tweetdeck.com). HootSuite and TweetDeck have the advantage of being web-based. Both platforms have free and paid versions. It is a good idea to start with the free versions of each before upgrading to one of their monthly plans. Both platforms offer statistic tracking such as how many Twitter users click links (must be created with the application) and Klout (clout) of Twitter users.

HootSuite and TweetDeck also have the ability to track other feeds from other social networks including Facebook and LinkedIn. Both also have fully functional smartphone apps available for research or updating on the go.

Choosing between platforms is really a matter of personal choice, and the platform you find most convenient to use based on your needs.

Monitoring Tweets

It is simple to set up keyword searches in one of these Twitter tools such as opponents' names, issues (e.g., abortion rights and the candidate's name, or even bodies of government). In order to keep up with popular keyword feeds, it is imperative that someone monitor the stream several times a day. This gives the campaign the ability to respond either via Twitter or via other channels in a real-time fashion.

Monitoring tweets is just one step to competitive listening. Campaigns should also use historic Twitter searches to derive information on opposing campaigns. Below are some of the tools available to conduct this research.

Google Search—For a period of time, Google had made real-time search of Twitter updates possible. In July 2011, the contract between Google and Twitter ended, but those who tweet for rankings, should take heart in the fact that Twitter activities such as the retweeting of articles, still has a positive effect on Google rankings. In fact, all social media activity can affect rankings. Plus, the launch of Google+, which plans to integrate all other social networks, will also have an impact should the platform and its plans to drive social media activity prove successful.

Topsy—This search engine boasts a Twitter archive back to August 2008. According to the site:

> Topsy is a realtime search engine powered by the Social Web. Unlike traditional web search engines, Topsy indexes and ranks search results based upon the most influential conversations millions of people are having every day about each specific term, topic, page or domain queried.[5]

The Power of Twitter Lists

Twitter lists are another tool to conduct competitive research on other candidates and their supporters. One of the key benefits of Twitter lists is that it is possible to follow a list without following the individual Twitter users. Investigate whether opponents are publicly listing supporters or influencers. The way to see their lists is illustrated in the screenshot below.

Twitter also allows for the creation of private lists. This is especially useful when segmenting opponents' followers, influencers, or donors. It is easy to see all of the activity of these lists by simply clicking on them. This is where Twitter tools such as HootSuite or TweetDeck become especially useful because they enable the user to view all list activity in a single feed. Listorious. com is another useful search tool for locating Twitter lists.

Hashtags—How Twitter Conversations Are Organized

Similar to lists are hashtags or Twitter's way of grouping similar conversations. Just like following Twitter lists, hashtags are a shortcut to finding information on a particular topic fast. For instance if there is a debate or conference, the organizers often designate a Twitter hashtag.

The Twitter hashtag is designated with a pound sign preceding the topic. For instance, in the search example below #economy returns real-time Twitter results for tweets pertaining to this keyword. Hhashtags can be set up as searches in either the HootSuite or TweetDeck for ongoing search based on specific keywords.

Figure 1 Hashtags are a simple way for Twitter users to group conversations on a topic such as the economy.

Using Twitter for Issue Research

One of the drawbacks of using Twitter as a competitive tool in a campaign is that (as of this writing) only about 8 percent of the American population actively uses Twitter.[6] However, it is an excellent research tool for news on issues, news and information on opponents. It is an especially useful tool for the following user demographics:

- Generation Y—Internet users between the ages of 18 and 29.
- African Americans and Latinos—These population groups (Internet users) are more than two times as likely to use Twitter as Caucasians.
- City dwellers—Residents of highly populated areas are more than twice as likely to be Twitter users as their more suburban or rural counterparts. (Source: Pew Research, 2010)

The methods for researching opponents outlined in the preceding sections can be applied to issue research. You can locate the influencers on particular topics by searching for the following information surrounding an issue:

- Company names (Fannie Mae and housing crisis, loan defaults)
- Initiative names (Energy conservation, health-care reform)
- Industry topics (Financial, health-care, manufacturing)
- Trends (Retirement savings, consumer spending)
- Breaking news (Layoffs, scandals, innovations)
- Individuals (Known influencers and what they are saying)

SlideShare—Find Presentations from Opponents and Research Issues

This site is a compilation of presentations (PowerPoint and webcasts) on just about any topic in business or research. The benefit of searching this site is to find information on trends and even presentations prepared or presented by opponents. One of the most popular uses of SlideShare (www.slideshare.com) is to offer analysis and predictions.

For instance, in the following screenshot, the presenters revealed how social media paid off for key candidates in Virginia in the 2009 election.[7] Such presentations can provide insights for how to prepare for upcoming races or see where opponents made mistakes in past elections.

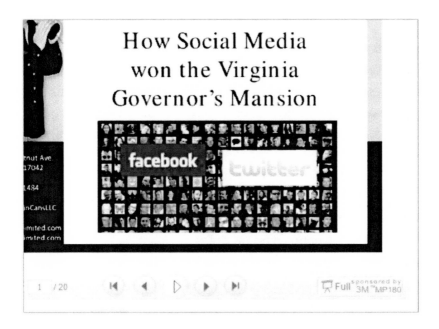

This site is also a powerful tool because presentations are available for download, meaning it is simple to store away presentations or information when conducting research. Also, look out for presentations from past conferences or rallies. Supporters sometimes share these as means of educating other voters.

Google Alerts—Monitor Virtually Any Electronic Resource on Opponents or Issues. This tool is a must-have to stay competitive in the political arena today. It is the most important tool a campaign has on social intelligence and it is the simplest to implement and monitor.

Google Alerts (www.google.com/alerts) can either be delivered via e-mail or feed reader. Although it is not possible to monitor Google Alerts at the present time in social media monitoring tools such as HootSuite or TweetDeck, Google's Reader (www.google.com/reader) makes monitoring multiple alerts easy to manage.

Each alert becomes a subscription in the Reader, so it is possible to scan alerts quickly.

Also, Google Alerts allows customization on sources including Web results, blogs, news, videos, or discussions. Alerts can be set up to notify "as it happens," "once a day" or "once a week." The time settings apply to email or the Reader. It is also possible to filter only the "best results."

Stay Abreast of Website Changes with RSS Feeds or with ChangeDetection.com Using an RSS/web change monitoring tool to detect what opponents are doing on their websites can offer additional insights to the campaign. RSS feeds or "Really Simple Syndication" is used to publish frequently updated works—such as blog entries, news headlines, audio, and video—in a standardized format".[8] RSS feeds are delivered to "readers" such as Google Reader via special software.

That is why Google Reader is a smart tool in any campaign's listening infrastructure. It is especially valuable in monitoring key changes to opponents' positioning statements or named supporters. Change detection websites such as the free ChangeDetection.com (www.changedetection.com) allow the user to view the before and after of any website update.

Investigate Campaign Financial Contributors

Knowing the backers of campaigns can be just as powerful as knowing the candidate's next move. Keep up with contributors to campaigns via the Federal Election Commission's database (http://www.fec.gov/finance/disclosure/disclosure_data_search.shtml). The database is segmented several ways to find data on the following:

- **Candidate and PAC/Party Summaries.** Search by candidate, committee, state, party, office, or name. Data from the past two Congressional election cycles is available in this database.
- **Individual Search.** Search by contributor name, city, state, ZIP code, principal business, date, or amount.
- **Committee Search.** Search for contributions received or made by a specific committee by name, city, state, ZIP code, Treasurer's name, party designation, or committee type.
- **Candidate Search.** Search for contributions received by a specific campaign using the candidate's name, state, or party affiliation.[9]

Researching Individuals—Supporters, Candidates and Influencers
Learning a person's contribution to the social scene is possible by locating the profiles on sites including LinkedIn, Twitter and their personal websites. However, according to social media experts Swigart and Campbell[10], aggregating that content in one place is often challenging, unless the person's name is unique.

Here are three resources to conduct more in-depth individual social searches:

NNDB.com
This website is a database of detailed information on individuals. Locating someone at the local level (unless they have served in office or have a public company background) may be challenging. However, it is a good resource for finding information on federal campaigns.

The database compiles data on every office, degree and even personal data such as church membership on persons of permanent public interest, holders of certain public offices, civic, or business positions (including board membership) and individuals with entries in selected works (movies, encyclopedias, etc.)[11].

Muckety Map (www.muckety.com)
This site is similar to NNDB.com, but it focuses more on relationships between people and organizations. It allows searches for people and organizations. The visual map provides both current (solid lines) and past affiliations (dotted lines) with organizations, people and legislation. The example below shows Bennie G. Thompson, chair of the Homeland Security Committee of the House of Representatives. He is linked to the financial bailout of 2008 and as shown in the following screenshot. Each topic with a "plus sign" is expandable to show the underlying connections. Highlighting (which can be seen in full-color online map) shows his connections to the financial market bailouts bill in 2008.

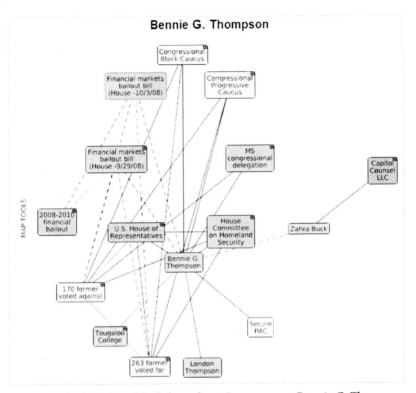

Figure 2. This "Muckety Map" shows how Congressman Bennie G. Thompson relates to current and past legislation, organizations and people. The dotted lines show past affiliations; solid are current affiliations (Muckety.com, 2010).

This tool is useful for deriving dates and connections in an easy-to-view format. It is also possible to simplify the maps by removing connections or information, if a researcher is looking to create a specific profile.

Muckety.com also gives a profile below the map of the official, businessperson, organization, or author, to name a few. Similar to NNDB, the site pulls information from the following sources: government agencies, state and federal courts, organization websites, news publications, books, and interviews.

Another useful tool available via Muckety.com is the news section of the site. It pulls headlines from across the Web to give up-to-date information on figures in its databases.[12]

Social Mention (www.socialmention.com)
This site works much like Google Alerts or Topsy, and is dedicated exclusively to social mentions including blogs, microblogs, social bookmarks, comments, events, images, news, video and audio content. Alerts from any or all of these mediums plus a search term can be sent via email daily or weekly.

It is also possible to see a figure's social influence, the top keywords, the strength of the subject, the person's influence in social media or even supporter passion for the candidate or issue via social media. In the following example, Mississippi Senator Roger Wicker has a one-percent strength of influence (discussions) in social media, while those discussing him are at a 42-percent "passion" level.

This tool, combined with many other measurement tools, can reveal how influential an opponent is in social circles online.

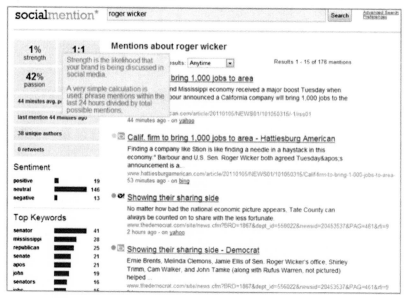

Wrapping Up Social Intelligence

Social media research tools help to provide campaigns with resources to investigate opponents, supporters, influencers, and issues associated with a campaign. The success of these resources is readily dependent on how engaged the candidate is, how engaged is the base of support, how influential the candidate is, the public's perspective on an individual or issue, and the timing of the research. This list is far from comprehensive as new technologies are emerging on a daily basis, but it should provide a foundation of the types of data available and ways to begin.

It is important to restate that a campaign team should evaluate the complexity of an election and combine social media research with traditional methods. In addition, those running for office or planning a campaign should also consider their voter target and validate that target's use of social technologies before diving into serious research.

More Resources to Consider in Researching Opponents and Issues:
The Fast Company Field Guide to Modern Political Campaigns
http://www.fastcompany.com/article/the-fast-company-field-guide-to-modern-political-campaigns

This guide makes some excellent points about how to gauge the social media presence of a campaign. Use the tactics mentioned and apply to competitive research to gain an even sharper picture of the opposition.

SmartBrief's CampaignGrid E-mail Newsletter
http://www.smartbrief.com/campaigngrid/index.jsp?campaign=signup_box

A monthly e-newsletter, SmartBrief's CampaignGrid provides a roundup of all the most relevant content on trends in technology and social media that affect candidates, causes and consultants in the political arena.

Post-Election Research

According to Jesse Stanchak, editor of the SmartBrief newsletter, it is important to gauge what the competition does after election night. While a politician's Facebook connections is far from the same as having more votes, still, Stanchak notes, "Several high-profile candidates with larger Facebook communities lost last night, but having the capacity to create and nurture those ties goes a long way toward keeping the base fired up," he says.[13]

Hence, though every candidate running seeks to win, the advent of social network support does mean the base of support can continue even beyond a loss.

This becomes a key lesson for candidates considering entering the next race. Staying engaged with what a losing candidate communicates to his or her base can give a potential candidate insight and strategy ideas long before the announcement of a follow-up race.

Facebook is one way to keep the base engaged. Quoting Ward, Stanchak writes that this communication platform is "being used to stoke the passions of true believers who will then go out and act as evangelists, rallying others to your side."[14]

This is important information for candidates who are looking ahead to the next election cycle. Mind the feeds of losing opponents to see who these "evangelists" are. Candidates who follow their feeds can garner an understanding of the overall campaign messages to come.

1 Mirman, E. (2010, November 8). Why You Should Link to Your Competitors—A Lesson from Yahoo. HubSpot Blog. Blog post retrieved from http://blog.hubspot.com/blog/tabid/6307/bid/7072/Why-You-Should-Link-to-Your-Competitors-A-Lesson-from-Yahoo.aspx

2 Alterian. (2010) Alterian SM2 Pre-Election Predictions More Accurate than Pundits; Press release retrieved from http://www.alterian.com/ourcompany/newsevents/news/social-election-predictions/

3 Stanchak, J. How Studying Politicians Can Make Your Brand's Social Media Campaign a Winner. Blog post retrieved from: http://smartblogs.com/socialmedia/2010/11/03/social-media-and-politics/ <"

4 Stanchak, J.

5 Topsy.com http://corp.topsy.com/

6 Smith, A. & Rainie, L. *Pew Research Center's Internet & American Life Project—Eight Percent of Americans Use Twitter*. Retrieved from http://www.pewinternet.org/Reports/2010/Twitter-Update-2010.aspx

7 Tin Cans Unlimited LLC. (2009). How Social Media Won the Virginia Governor's Race [Electronic presentation]. Retrieved from http://www.slideshare.net/TinCans/how-social-media-won-the-virginia-governors-race

8 Webopedia, (2010). http://www.webopedia.com/TERM/R/RSS.html

9 Federal Election Commission. (2010). Disclosure Data Search. Retrieved from: http://www.fec.gov/finance/disclosure/disclosure_data_search.shtml

10 Swigart, S., & Campbell S. (2010) Go Beyond Google: Gathering Internet Intelligence. USA

11 NNDB.com; Bennie Thompson. Retrieved from: http://www.nndb.com/people/707/000040587/.

12 Muckety.com; Bennie G. Thompson. Retrieved from: http://www.muckety.com/Bennie-G-Thompson/117.muckety

13 Stanchak, J.

14 Stanchak, J.

CHAPTER 8

Fundraising Strategies

W HILE THE OBAMA campaign[1] brought the strategic use of social media to the forefront, it is not the only instance in which social media has proven to be an effective way to create successful political outcomes for candidates. Social media has infused political campaigns with real and effective action using text messages, Twitter, Facebook fan pages, and more.

As mainstream America continues to adopt the use of social media into their everyday routines, local, state, and federal campaign elections are using social media as part of the tactics for capturing the attention of voters. Without the use of social media as part of their fundraising strategies, politicians may experience the opposite effect, which is a loss of opportunity to utilize another source of campaign contributions designed to build a strong foundation of support.

Be careful about assuming that certain demographics of supporters and potential supporters are not using social media. In fact, all age groups and ethnicities are engaged in social media to some degree or another, and one of the fastest growing groups is women over the age of 55. In a 60-day period, Facebook users almost doubled, which offers huge potential for reaching your audience—no matter who they are.

Political campaigns should plan to include social media efforts as part of their baseline strategies. These include the use of the politicians' website, a Facebook page, and mobile applications such as text messages.

Political campaign managers must weigh how these online fundraising and campaigning efforts affect offline fundraising results, such as the number of invitations that go out for fundraising events. In addition, if the politician is asking for money on social media networks and donors give, the campaign must determine often it will return to the donors—be it online or offline—to ask for additional donations. All are areas to ponder when infusing social media efforts into political campaigns.

Champion Choice

Current networking trends are opening up new campaigning possibilities, and many campaigns are rushing to tap into new online networks to raise awareness, organize groups, and generate funds. With the ongoing adoption of social media by the mainstream, upcoming elections at the local, state, and federal level must arm themselves with a new set of tactics designed to capture voters' attention. Indeed, campaigns that do not utilize the web risk losing out on vital campaign contributions, not to mention growing and mobilizing a strong base of support. Because social media is generated by external influences, it tends to create a fresh awareness and stir a desire to bring about real change, naturally lending itself to innovation in business and politics; a chance to define a brand on the most personal of terms.

Obama was the first major-party candidate to reject taxpayers' money for the general election by declining public financing and the spending limits that came with it.1 He never even ran a formal fundraiser. His campaign proved that the strategic use of social media could propel a political campaign. In the month of February 2008, only one year after officially launching his campaign, Obama raised $55 million, $45 million of which was raised online.[2]

If you're not familiar with social media, it can be difficult to define. Similar to antiquated communication instruments such as a print periodical or a radio, social media is also a form of communication designed to engage. Where other forms of media primarily produce outgoing information, social media interacts with its users. If you're a web user, chances are, you've already been a part of this contemporary discourse. By posting a comment on an online news article, voting on an opinion poll, or browsing rating-generated "recommendations" on a Netflix account, you're interacting with Web 2.0 and changing the way it interacts with you.[3]

According to the Pew Internet & American Life Project, nearly half of all Americans have expressed their opinions in a public forum—blogs or social networking sites that provide new opportunities for this type of engagement.[4] Millions of Internet users access sites such as Facebook and YouTube to interact, exchange opinions, organize groups, and share audio and visual media. On Facebook alone, there are over 160 million objects that people interact with (pages, groups and events) every day.[5] So "Like" it or not, the Internet is now a part of everyday civic life.

Make It Easy

But let's face it. Social media is a broad term and it unsurprisingly covers a large range of websites. The common characteristic of a social media site is the user's ability to interact with the website as well as other visitors. As you consider implementing social media into a campaign, you must be aware of three major categories: Social News, Social Networking, and Social Photo and Video Sharing.

Social News—Allows users to interact by voting for articles and commenting on them. Popularly used sites include but are not limited to BayCitizen, Digg[6] and Propeller. During your campaign you may want to utilize these sites to peruse media portrayal of your candidate and gain a sense of public opinion.

Social Networking—Users interact by adding friends, commenting on profiles, joining groups and having discusssions. Facebook, MySpace, and Twitter are some popular examples. These sites can be a great way to gain awareness, organize groups or fundraise.

Social Photo and Video Sharing—Lets users interact by sharing photos or videos and commenting on user submissions. YouTube and Flickr are commonly used. These sites are perfect for creating a solid brand while allowing your supporters to follow your campaign events.

Global Snapshot: Russia's Blue Bucket Movement

Moscow residents were frustrated about Russia's double standard for the rich and powerful by allowing them to use flashing blue lights on the roofs of their luxury cars to drive in special lanes, go the wrong way and ignore speed limits and red lights. To appease their frustrations, they video taped various incidents between the blue light driven vehicles and the average driver, posting the videos online.

In addition, at the suggestion of Alexei Dozorov, head of the Moscow chapter of the Committee to Protect Drivers' Rights, Moscow protesters attached blue plastic buckets to the roofs of their cars to attract attention, hoping to make laughing stocks out of the people who use blue lights.

Radio host Sergei Parkhomenko took to his blog and urged drivers to do the same. On April 18, 2010, 50 bucket-topped cars drove around Moscow. Two days later, a band of motorists gathered to protest, but were stopped by police before they could begin.

Authorities attempted to fine drivers for violating "cargo transportation regulations." Two protesters were arrested April 20 for not taking their buckets down. They weren't arrested for breaking the cargo law but for disobeying a police order.

Investigations by Russian media revealed hundreds more blue light cars than the officially known some 960. A bill has been introduced in the State Duma that would fine drivers who abused their blue lights.

The Russian Car Owners Federation started a campaign with "Flashing Lights Are Russia's Shame" as its motto. Friends in high places joined their cause, and Moscow Mayor Yury Luzhkov told the Kommersant newspaper that aside from the president, prime minister and patriarch of the Russian Orthodox Church, nonemergency vehicles should not have flashing blue lights.

Dorzorov gathered a significant online following with "Blue Bucket" societies, whose members posted videos and pictures of their blue bucket exploits. Dorzorov remarked that people were fed up and wanted to fight back.

Through online content sharing, fighting back meant taking their plight to officials in a new way and thus, finding both empowerment and resolution.

Marquardt, Alexander. "Drivers Use Buckets to Fight Russian Double Standards."
abcnews.go.com. http://abcnews.go.com/print?id=10486616. April 27, 2010
http://continentsmith.blogspot.com/2010/05/russian-blue-bucket-protest.html.
http://rt.com/Top_News/2010-05-24/blue-bucket-climbed-car.html#.
http://www.russiandogs.net/blue-buckets-vs-migalki.html.
http://www.guardian.co.uk/world/2010/may/28/russia-moscow-blue-buckets-cars/
print.
http://www.themoscowtimes.com/vedomosti/article/editorial-blue-bucket-campaign-
prompts-excessive-new-law/406978.html.

By creating profiles or platforms on these social sites, candidates provide a forum not only for users to gain knowledge about the candidacy issues, but also a space to interact with other supporters. Users who participate in these groups are often positively affected, feeling personally involved in a candidate's campaign. Often the sheer experience of watching member growth can produce a sense of excitement and constant community that inspires current members to help gain more supporters.

To optimize your online efforts, some of the top strategies to consider as you explore the possibilities of social media in your campaign are as follows:

Widgets. Customization is important for all social networking profiles. Users want to share their opinions on a public forum. That's why supporters often independently spread and share campaign tools. Widgets, or short pieces of code, can be created to offer users the ability to download "plug-ins" such as customized local search engines, weather, instant messaging, airline ticket reservations, stock tickers, and a range of software applications. Most of these can be installed by simply cutting and pasting the embeddable content directly into a website.[7] For example, iGoogle, which many people set as their homepage, offers a wide range of widgets that can be added to the page so that whether you want your daily horoscope or dinner reservations, the content can be accessed directly. Widgets can be placed on a Facebook or other social networking site as well.

So, for example, you might add a "John Smith for Mayor. Donate Now." widget to your Facebook page so that others can donate to the candidate you recommend.

Badges and widgets make it easy for donors to raise money for their favorite causes on their websites, social networking pages and blogs. Widgets give anyone the opportunity to put the high-value services and content of the Web's leading companies directly on their own site. All you need to do is make them available. Software-as-a-service companies such as SalesForce.com make it easy to coordinate your marketing activities online. However it is important to consider how cost effective these sites will be depending on the size of your campaign.

Donors Voice and Choice. Donors want more say and more accountability when it comes to where their donations go. This means the process of giving has to become more personal. Organizations such as DonorsChoose[8] literally display what donor contributions will accomplish. Whether it is for a billboard in an individual's hometown or the simply donating the cost of printing flyers for your candidate's next rally, give your supporters a chance to be able to point to a physical representation of their donation.

Many donors are also looking for non-biased information from peers on candidates and campaigns. This often comes in the form of personal blogs or online discussion forums. Consider providing links to blogs of supporters or flattering news articles on your social networking profiles. By pursuing a search engine for your candidate's name, you might be surprised at what you can find.

Navigation. Investing in search engines is also a crucial component in directing potential voters to your campaign. For those interested individuals who search for the candidate on a site such as Google, it is important to make sure they will find the official site before any other media coverage: good, bad, or indifferent. The key is directing potential voters to a location at which they can learn about your candidate's opinions with regard to the issues. If the site speaks to potential donors' interests and answers their questions, they may think about getting involved. Make sure they have an opportunity to do so in the same place.

Currently, campaigning candidates are not embarrassed when it comes to asking for money. Online users expect everything to work as easily as a finely tuned search engine. Campaigns should be sure their website is simple to navigate. Maps (particularly those that visitors can add to or update) can effectively demonstrate great messages—from local party headquarters to the location of your candidate's next event. After all, accessibility is the major benefit of Internet resources, so make it even easier for individuals to donate by providing a link on every page of your campaign website. If you've visited either the Democrat or Republican party websites recently, you couldn't have missed the inconspicuous red buttons located on the top, right corner of every home page reading "Donate Now" or "Contribute."

You will also notice with many donation websites that there are no navigation elements on the page. In essence this forces the visitor to either press the "back" button on the Internet browser or change the web address manually. It is unclear whether this design technique is effective or simply aggravating to online visitors but it certainly accomplishes the goal of obtaining more screen time with potential voters.

Video. Video can tell a story like no other medium, giving viewers a sense of your candidate's charisma and core message. With the use of music or camera angles, video can generate an emotional response from your audience. Moreover, videos give you a solid chance to create an authentic brand. Campaigns are creating videos and encouraging supporters to make their own to tell their stories. Many times this comes in the form of past politicians and celebrities.

For example, Alan Grayson of Florida launched a fundraising campaign for his Congressional reelection to in spring 2010. He set a goal of $450,000 and by the end date, he had surpassed this goal by more than $20,000. His success may have something to do with the YouTube videos embedded on his campaign website. When visitors first enter the site, a video of Howard Dean automatically plays, expressing his deep respect for the man personally and professionally. Political filmmaker Michael Moore passionately endorses Grayson while he greets visitors entering the contribution link. "Do what you can to support him. And, I'll do the same," says Moore—just another nudge to complete the transaction.[9]

Multi-Channel Resources. Door-to-door campaigning can be an effective way to introduce your candidate into communities. But in addition to undertaking the "kissing babies and shaking hands" approach, campaigning committees are realizing there are simple, and more effective ways of establishing a personal connection with the public. Smart campaigns are coordinating online/offline efforts to maximize return on investment, as multichannel donors are more valuable and more loyal.

Amidst the 2004 primary election, Democratic candidate Howard Dean was investigating the possibilities of using the Internet to his benefit. By following individual blogs and finding common critiques, his campaign committee was able to tweak everything from his lexicon to his public policy, creating a real discourse with potential voters. But rather than using the Internet as just a constant opinion poll, Dean enlisted the help of Meetup.

com, which boasts it is the world's largest network of local groups. Through this site, Dean was able to organize a throng of volunteers going door-to-door, writing personal letters to likely voters, hosting meetings, and distributing campaign flyers. Clearly, virtual support translates to real, active support.[10]

Sustained Giving. Beyond having the capability of managing online monthly donations, campaigns are designing websites for attracting and retaining sustainer donors. Political party and individual candidate donation forms are becoming extremely well designed, providing convenient, easy-to-view form fields. If you've already registered on the site, it repopulates your information, saving donors the time of filling out their name, address, ZIP code and phone number. If the transaction was quick and easy, donors are more likely to give again.

The Republican National Committee website provides a space for ongoing support by requiring donors to choose a payment plan. Their long-term option automatically subtracts the same fee from their debit or credit card on a monthly basis until a request for cancellation is made.[11]

Major donors. Contrary to popular belief, large donors do go online. They will research candidates and the positions they hold, and their first impressions may come from a candidate's website. Many want to make their donations online—some even make large gifts to earn promotional credit card perks.

Beyond the "Donate Now" Button

Keeping fundraising fresh and exciting for potential contributors can be difficult at times. And with so many candidates online it can even be tough to stand out in the crowd. It is important to keep in mind that donors tend to respond to fun, personal, albeit quirky fundraisers.

Justin Flippen, candidate for Florida State Representative created a Twitter, Facebook, and Flickr account he shared media—everything from the events he had attended to the status of a family pet's surgery. All profiles are all linked to his campaign website. In May 2010, he invited members of his online committee to donate over $5,000 within the span of two weeks. A short-window fundraiser may sound severe, but Flippen's campaign committee did something extremely effective. Using the candidate's birth date, 5-6-78, they set the goal of $5,678. He wasn't just asking his supporters to contribute to his campaign, he was asking for a birthday gift. Avid supporters who visited any of his social media platform sites felt compelled to donate during this timeframe.[12]

Whether he met the goal remains unclear—though he did lose the election to incumbent -Gwyndolyn Clarke-Reed—Flippen employed clever fundraising tactics that put the "fun" back in "fundraising"—a technique we will see more and more of as candidates strive to humanize themselves to voters.

Going Mobile. Mobile Giving websites such as mobilecause. com, Causecast, and mGive, are tapping into the phone market, exponentially increasing their outreach demographics. Fundraising has become as easy as sending a text message to give any donation amount. Technology blog Gearlog reports that according to the CTIA-Wireless Association while only 30% of Americans subscribe to Internet access, over 250 million Americans now subscribe to a cellular-phone service.[13] Campaign accounts can be set up through these websites, and cost an average of $99 per month. However, they often pay for themselves. In 2010, over the course of three weeks, mGive processed over $37 million in donations for Haiti, proving that fundraising can be just as effective through text message as through any other medium.[14]

Don't Overlook the Basics

Just because you're new to some of the strategies of campaign fundraising don't be fooled into thinking you should now throw all of your other experiences aside. At the end of the day, regardless of the medium, fundraising must focus on building trust and attending to the donor. Your online and strategies should focus on cultivating relationships, one donor at a time. If you understand fundraising in an offline environment, you will be far better suited to apply this knowledge to the digital fundraising space.

As you consider these strategy guidelines and begin to explore the world of social media, bear in mind a few common pitfalls. As with other types of fundraising, online solicitations must be registered with the appropriate officials. Check with your state attorney's office or secretary of state office to find out the requirements in your region.

And do not overlook security. Online donations and transactions are becoming commonplace around the world. Consumer confidence in doing business online is rapidly growing. However, don't take security lightly. Identity theft is still rampant and the online space is filled with serious considerations to protect against. PayPal[15] or Click and Pledge offer the highest level of security: full system redundancy, 128-bit encryption, advanced virus protection and controlled access to credit card information.[16] Whichever service you use, be sure it is also in compliance with the strict security standards enforced by major credit card companies.

As the population of Internet users continues to expand, it is imperative that you have an online presence with the ability to accept campaign donations and manage events. Remember that Internet users tend to be more actively interested in news and politics and they enjoy taking a much deeper examination of a candidate's policies, beliefs, and plans. Be sure to involve them by offering opportunities for them to contribute online to your campaign—this may mean the difference between a concession and a winning campaign.

1 Summary Data for Barack Obama | OpenSecrets. OpenSecrets.org: Money in Politics—See Who's Giving & Who's Getting. Center for Responsive Politics, 13 July 2009. Web. (2010, 20 May) http://www.opensecrets.org/pres08/summary.php?id=n00009638>."

2 Obama Raises $55 Million in February, Sets New Record. Online Posting. CNN.com. Cable News Network, Turner Broadcasting System, Inc., 6 Mar. 2008. Web. (2010, 10 May). http://www.cnn.com/2008/POLITICS/03/06/democrats.campaign/index.html>."

3 Netflix: Rent as Many Movies as You Want for Only $8.99 a Month! Free Trial. Web. (2010, 10 May). <http://netflix.com>.

4 The State of Civic Engagement in America. The Pew Internet and American Life Project, 2010. Web. (2010, 10 May). "http://www.pewinternet.org/Reports/2009/15--The-Internet-and-Civic-Engagement/2-"-The-Current-State-of-Civic-Engagement-in-America.aspx?r=1>.

5 Facebook Statistics. Welcome to Facebook. Web. (2010, 10 May). http://www.facebook.com/facebook?ref=pf/r.php?locale=en_US#!/press/info.ph"p?statistics>.

6 Digg—The Latest News Headlines, Videos and Images. Web. (2010, 12 May). http://digg.com.

7 CRM—Salesforce.com. Web. (2010, 10 May). http://SalesForce.com.

8 DonorsChoose.org: An Online Charity Connecting You to Classrooms in Need. 2010. Web. (2010, 14 May). <http://www.donorschoose.org/>.

9 Donate to A Congressman With Guts: Alan Grayson. Perf. Michael Moore. Home | Alan Grayson for U.S. Congress. The Committee to Elect Alan Grayson. Web. (2010, 12 May). https://www.graysonforcongress.com/donate.asp?s=cwg1>."

10 Overby, Peter. Dean Makes New Fundraising Push Online. Weblog post. Dean Makes New Fundraising Push Online. NPR, (2003, 28 July) Web. (2010, 14 May). "http://www.npr.org/templates/story/story.php?storyId=1359875".

11 Donate Today - Republican National Committee. Web. (2010, 13 May). <https://donate.gop.com/>.

12 Vote Justin Flippen on August 24th! Justin S. Flippen, Democrat, for State Representative, (2010, 3 May). Web. (2010, 20 May). <http://www.justinflippen.com/Justin_Flippen_for_Florida_State_House_92/Campaign_News/Entries/2010/5/3_Shhhhhits_JUSTINS_BIRTHDAY-_the_Birthday_Fundraising_Challenge!.html>.

13 U.S. Cell-Phone Penetration Tops 82 Percent. Web log post. Gearlog. Ziff Davis Media, (2007,13 November). Web. (2010, 11 May). http://www.gearlog.com/2007/11/us_cellphone_penetration_tops.php.

14 Joos, Stephen. Behind the Scenes at MGive- Processing Over $37 Million in Donations. Web log
     post. MGive Blog. MGive, (2010, 3 February). Web. (2010, 12 May)
     "http://blog.mgive.com/2010/02/03/behind-the-scenes-at-mgive-processing-over-37-million-
     in-donations/".

15 Security Tools - PayPal. Send Money, Pay Online or Set Up a Merchant Account with PayPal.
     PayPal. Web. (2010, 20 May). "https://www.paypal.com/cgi-bin/webscr?cmd=xpt/Marketing/
     securitycenter/general/FreeTools-outside".

16 Click & Pledge Privacy Statement. Online Fundraising Software | Donor Management Software |
     Online Donation | Click & Pledge. Web. (2010, 20 May). <http://clickandpledge.com/privacy/>.

CHAPTER 9

Online Whistle-Stop Tour:
Campaign Channels

OLD-FASHIONED TOWNHALL meetings are rapidly becoming a thing of the past with the various types of social media being made ever more accessible to the masses. In a society of jam-packed candidate and constituent schedules, many politicians are beginning to use the Internet and social media to enhance communications with constituents and to help promote constituent engagement among members of their community.

Technology and social media are enhancing our democracy in a very big way by bringing citizens closer to their government. Technologies are giving power to the people. So, in order for governments to ensure authority and relevance, they must act quickly to meet the rising expectations for openness, accountability, effectiveness, and efficiency in the public arena.

Consider social media outlets as two-way streets that give the ability to communicate and define activities that pull together technology, social interaction, and creating content.

The Online Townhall

According to teletownhall.com, a very simple form of digital technology allows townhall meetings to utilize voice over IP (Internet Protocol) along with a mass-automated, variable-speed dialing system. In simple terms, this technology enables the system to dial out to thousands of phone numbers from a pre-selected list with very little cost. The tele-townhall is a virtual townhall meeting that enables a candidate or politician to make live, direct contact with tens of thousands of voters at one designated time by simply using the telephone— whether it is a cell phone or landline.

The speaker simply logs on to a simple web interface which controls the event through a web browser. Once the event begins, the system automatically dials out to a pre-determined list of households. A pre-recorded message will play for every person who answers the phone. They will be invited to remain on the phone to participate in a tele-townhall with the guest speaker. Until the dialing process is complete, participants will be connected to a live event in progress.

Any participant who wishes to ask a question can press "zero" and will be entered into a queue. Call screeners may be used to speak with callers prior to allowing them to talk with the speaker. The speaker has the capability to allow or disallow participants to ask questions live during the conference.

Detailed reporting and statistics are very beneficial. Once the event is over, results are returned, which include participants, non-participants, fax machines, answering machines, busy signals and other indicators. Data are also provided for the participants, which show how long each participant remained on the phone, if the participant interacted with the speaker with a question, and how a participant responded to polls conducted. All of this data can be saved and imported into contact tracking systems. This data can then be used to select participants for future events. This will allow future events to be targeted specifically for a particular type of audience.

An unlimited number of polling questions can be configured prior to the event and any of those questions can be posed live to participants during the conference. Responses are received by pressing specific numbers on their phone keypads that correspond to the answers previously configured. Results of the polling questions are displayed in real time on the speaker's web interface and are retained for further review. This is important while doing message testing as it can be targeted toward a specific group before taking their core messages to larger groups.

Guest speakers can be invited to join the tele-townhall event from practically anywhere in the world. Participants have the option of transferring instantly from the conference to a department, district office or live call center by pressing a button on their phone keypad. This feature can be used to collect email addresses, accept donations, or to answer a participant's specific question which may be too personal to be heard by the entire audience.

Global Snapshot: 2010 Mexico Election

Mexico's July 4, 2010 single-round gubernatorial election in the state of Veracruz was so close that representatives of the *Partido Revolucionario Intitucional* (PRI) agreed to allow electoral votes opened and counted one by one to confirm that candidate Javier Duarte won outright.

Miquel Angel Yunes Linares, "Viva Veracruz" coalition candidate, states that he was a victim of electoral fraud and requested the recount. The PRI agreed to the recount on the condition that the losing candidate would no longer refer to himself as the "legitimate governor."

According to Jason Marczak, Director of Policy at *Americas Society & Council of the Americas*, the Federal Election Institute (IFE) in Mexico has played a critical role in ensuring free and fair voting in federal elections.

"Mexico has made important strides in laying the groundwork for a clean electoral process," said Marczak. "Candidates' news coverage is even monitored to ensure an equitable balance among candidates."

Social media was not absent during the campaigns. The Interactive Advertising Bureau reports that there are over 30 million Mexicans—of a population of 110 million—with access to the Web, and about 14 million people belong to social networks.

"One of the things that was done in the 2010 elections was 'citizen monitoring' through social media,' said Marczak. "This allowed for any questionable practices to be immediately reported throughout the process."

Alianza Civica, a group that coordinated strategies of observing the July 4th elections, focused on the states of Hidalgo, Oaxaca, Puebla, and Veracruz. The group worked with approximately 120 organizations, in that they set up a platform for citizens to send complaints toward the electoral process.

Social media was utilized via e-mail, SMS, mobile telephones, Twitter and Facebook.

Jason Marczak, Director of Policy, *Americas Society & Council of the Americas*, (212) 277-8384, jmarczak@as-coa.org
BBC News. *"Q&A: Mexico Election." news.bbc.co.uk. "<http://news.bbc.co.uk/2/hi/ americas/5114662.stm.>"*
"<http://www.presidencia.gob.mx/index.php?DNA=26>".
"<http://en.wikipedia.org/wiki/Mexican_general_election,_2006.>"
"<http://www.envio.org.ni/utils/imprimir>".

At the conclusion of the conference, participants who did not have the opportunity to ask their questions live during the event can go to the TTH voice center where personal messages can be left for later review.

Participants also have the option of dialing into a toll-free telephone number that is distributed prior to the event and join the conference. Staff members, press, and other VIPs are also assigned a phone number so they may listen to the event as well.

Easy-to-read detailed reports are sent to the speaker after the meeting which includes detailed statistics to use for current and future analysis. According to Broadnet's TeleForum, a company that provides the technology for tele-townhall meetings, they "deliver an average 16-minute attention span—more than 18 times the average stay of a web viewer and 38 times more than the attention focused on television advertising spots." The tele-townhall meeting proves to be very effective, with a majority of the population owning cell phones, people can join in from practically anywhere. Coupled with the average attention span of the participants and low cost, these factors make this method a key strategy in reaching constituents.

Townhall meetings are also being held online where the speaker can be seen and heard via live streaming video. Participants simply log on from their own computer via an Internet connection and web browser. This method is highly successful in building positive relationships between constituents and the participants. It also bridges the gap for a large portion of the population who own computers but have done away with the traditional home telephone and do not own a cell phone.

Video and web conferencing software is revolutionizing the way politics is conducted by taking it to a whole new level. The process is as simple as logging on to a particular website at a designated time. Participants are greeted with a screen of introductory information and a moderator is there to assist if the participants experience any technical difficulties. Questions are typically submitted via chat and are put into a queue after being reviewed by a moderator's assistant. The speaker can answer the questions via live video and audio, audio only, or through chat sessions.

As an added benefit, younger generations can be reached online as they spend a significant amount of time in this space. Reaching out to young voters will raise awareness and educate them on important issues as well as educating them on the importance of voting.

Online Town Hall Meetings: Exploring Democracy in the 21st Century summarizes the findings and recommendations from an academic study of 21 online townhall meetings between Members of Congress and their constituents, according to cmfweb.org. According to the report, the townhalls "increased engagement, probability of voting and found the discussions to be of high quality."

"The meetings also increased member approval and attracted a diverse array of constituents. Research indicated that "95 percent agreed (79 percent strongly agreed) that they would be interested in doing similar online sessions for other issues." [1]

"Conducting online meetings with constituents offers Members of Congress a flexible tool for communication in addition to the traditional in-person meetings, tele-townhalls and newsletters," said Beverly Bell, Executive Director of the Congressional Management Foundation. "Our research shows that people like hearing from— and feeling heard by—their representatives in all formats, including online." [2]

Online and tele-townhall meetings have both proven to be successful for many reasons. The cost for an event is minimal and participants are able to interact without having to leave the comfort of home. This is a huge incentive for those with small children or the disabled to take part in these meetings. And, participants not willing to ask questions in a public arena are more likely to ask them via telephone or Internet.

Tweet, Post, and Update Your Platform

Twitter is another front runner among the social media powerhouses used by politicians to reach thousands of people within seconds. The influence and power of tweets have been covered throughout this book and with good reason.

Some argue that Twitter is not a social network, *per se*. Still, the growing number of users puts it on comparable terms with the seemingly unstoppable Facebook, which is heading toward one billion users.

While most experts believe that Twitter will not sway votes in any significant way, it is an important part of social media. Not only is it a free tool, it can be used to respond to attacks by opponents in an instant. It is also a good tool to use for announcing upcoming events which have the potential to increase fund raising success and post thoughts of the day.

Another advantage to tweeting is that it is an effective way to send out information related to opponents who may make defamatory statements. This gives the opponent the ability to respond immediately. The simplicity of Twitter makes it quite appealing to those who aren't as technically savvy as others.

The possible negative effects include politicians "tweeting" too quickly—or tweeting inappropriately—without giving some thoughts to their statement and its consequence. As in all political arenas, statements made can be used against political candidates just as simply as they can be used for them. While Twitter does not offer the same integrated video and audio features of real-time web conferencing, it can get links to this content out in an instant, with the potential to reach millions.

GovTwit is the largest directory which provides official government Twitter IDs on state, local, and federal levels. The site also offers directory updates via Twitter that are tweeted as they are made and also offer a Facebook fan page you may join. Twitter is growing and so is its utility, which may then support a wider range of communications applications in the future.

Facebook, the largest social networking website, is the most widely used form of social media used by politicians and political campaigns. It is a platform that can allow voters to connect quickly and easily by creating a simple Facebook page. Pages are a valuable tool for posting information and updates to keep political supporters up to date on a variety of issues. Candidate support can increase by spreading the word to friends of supporters and will continue to grow over time. Encouraging appropriate content behavior by establishing a comment policy for your page is an important consideration as you are developing your Facebook strategy.

Another great tool available on Facebook is a calendar where upcoming events that will be held for campaigning efforts or public speaking engagements can be posted far in advance. Invitations can be sent to all of the supporters and they can reply whether they will be attending the event or not. This is a valuable tool when in the planning stages for your event.

Photos of local events and links to other sites such as the main campaign website can be posted, and pictures and video may also be uploaded via mobile device. A date and time can be scheduled for a Facebook townhall meeting and the site will allow you to painlessly send out bulk e-mails to all of your supporters to increase participation. These e-mails can then be forwarded by your current supporters to their friends and increase awareness.

Supporters would log on at the specified time and may ask questions on the wall page. These questions are able to be filtered before they are allowed to appear. Once approved, the candidate will then have the opportunity to respond.

Responding in a timely manner to questions, comments, and wall posts proves to the supporters that their thoughts, ideas, and concerns are important and valued. Facebook gives politicians and political campaigns and organizations an opportunity to receive immediate feedback on various topics and issues. This is a great opportunity for message testing as you can send polls out to a distinct group of supporters and analyze the data following the submissions by the supporters.

Most importantly, promotion of a Facebook page is crucial to its effectiveness. The Facebook username can be posted in many places. Links can be posted on websites, in emails and campaign brochures, on signage, t-shirts, and at campaign headquarters. Supporters should be encouraged to add a badge to their blog or website to show who they support and possibly influence friends and family to take a closer look at the candidate.

Another popular social networking site is YouTube, the popular, free video-sharing website which lets users upload, view, and share video clips.

Townhall meetings can easily be posted online for those to view that were unable to attend in person. According to newmediacampaigns.com, "The service's search engine is second in use only to Google. This staggering number of searches makes it essential to own your candidate's name for search on this platform."[3]

The downside to YouTube is that anyone can post video, which ultimately means if a candidate is caught in a compromising or unflattering scenario, this, too, can be posted to the site where it is seen by millions.

Emerging Platforms

While Twitter and Facebook are political favorites, more platforms continue to emerge. In April 2010, Microsoft released TownHall which is a social media platform designed to further serve the needs of political figures. According to msdn.com, "TownHall is an ideal tool for politicians and other public officials who want to host online social experiences that drive richer discussion around top interests and concerns with the American public. Think of it as software that allows you to easily create a destination for folks to voice opinions, identify problems, offer solutions and come together around common interests and concerns." [4]

Another resource aimed directly at politicians and constituents is 20dc.com. According to its website, "20DC is the first step in the future of politics. The way we elect candidates, organize action, disperse information and even fundraise is changing as fast as Internet technology develops. 20DC has a vast array of features that allow for political discussion and organization— all in one place and all online.

"The content of the site is created and controlled by users. After all, it wouldn't be much of a site about popular democracy otherwise, would it?" The site also includes a Townhall feature. [5]

In January 2008, Facebook's effect on the American political system became clear. The site teamed up with ABC and Saint Anselm College which offered users to provide live feedback with regard to the "back to back" January 5 Republican and Democratic debate. Debate groups were organized around specific topics such as register to vote, and message questions that Facebook users took part in. The Facebook application "US Politics" was installed by over 1 million people in order to take part. This proved that Facebook is an extremely powerful new way to interact and voice opinions with constituents. The Facebook effect has definitely affected youth voting and candidate support.

Social networks for politicians inform constituents and forms communities around specific interests. The majority of the population has seen social networking used to send some powerful messages. It is obvious due to the fact that hundreds of thousands of people are speaking their minds on Facebook, Twitter, blogs, candidate websites and elsewhere. Laptops, smartphones, and other gadgets are no longer luxuries but business tools used by many. They are the new mobile townhall.

In the U.S., hundreds of elected officials and candidates, from city mayors to President Obama, are now regularly using the new technologies available, which has boosted favorability ratings by at least a 10 percent margin, while educating and motivating supporters and raising funds. However, the reality is that many agencies perceive and treat the use of social media as a technology issue, instead of a communications tool. The result is that management decisions are often based solely on technology considerations.

In many cases, the focus is more on what can't be done rather than what can be done. The default approach should be openness and transparency. For this reason, government agencies need to be prepared that the decision to use social media will have significant impacts on the organizational culture in government. Currently, that threat of change could be impeding the embrace of social media by some government agencies.

One proposed solution would be to communicate a government-wide strategy for using social media tools to create a more effective, transparent, and cost-effective government. Given the budget constraints, this direction could gain appeal.

Many voters claim that social media can never replace a handshake and a face-to-face chat with someone wanting to run for a political office. It is always good to look someone in the eye, hear positions firsthand, and develop a sense of character. You can't do that as easily through a telephone or a computer monitor.

Voters don't want to lose the true essence of meeting someone that they may vote for in an election. While it is clear that the new technologies that exist today can definitely assist with a campaign by providing additional tools to reach constituents, promote campaigns and fundraising, release important information, and let voters know about important dates and events, this cannot replace the feet-on-the-ground hallmarks of any good campaign.

Therefore, candidates should never vacate the campaign trail and hide behind technology. Just as we have online dating sites, it's that first date when you really get to know the person. You may spend a few weeks or so talking by phone, e-mailing, or texting, but eventually you want to meet in person to ensure you like what you see. The dating site and interim communications are just initial engagement tools to bring two people together. So, too, is this the case in the voter-candidate relationship.

It is quite evident that it takes more than accessing new media sites and tools to make things happen in a campaign. And using them improperly may cause more harm than stumbling over a question at a press conference or performing poorly in a live, televised debate.

The Internet relentlessly continues to allow voters to become closer to politicians and law makers using various methods. The Internet can also be powerful and disruptive. In the end, a campaign is a campaign, and social media sites are merely enhancements that can put a campaign over the top if used properly and effectively. But importantly, they cannot be used successfully in isolation. And while social media can connect new pipelines of voters, donors, and prospective supporters, it does have its limitations—it can't shake your hand.

1 Lazer, D., Neblo, M., Esterling, K., Goldschmidt, K., & Burden, C. *Online Town Hall Meetings: Exploring Democracy in the 21st Century. ISBN: 1-930473-12-5. (2009). Congressional Management Foundation, Harvard Kennedy School, Northeastern University, University of California-Riverside. "<http://nposoapbox.s3.amazonaws.com/cmfweb/Online-Town-Hall-Meetings-Report.pdf.>"*

2 New Study Finds That Internet Town Hall Meetings Increase Constituent Trust, Perception of Lawmakers. (2010, 24 April). http://www.congressfoundation.org/index.php?option=com_cont ent&task=view&id=299&Itemid=50

3 Schossow, Clay. *"Using Social Media in Political Campaigns".* Newmediacampaigns.com. "<http://www.newmediacampaigns.com/page/using-social-media-in-political-campaigns. September 24, 2009.)>"

4 Kyle, Bruce. *"Microsoft Offers Political Town Hall Software for Windows Azure".* blogs.msdn.com. (2010, 24 April). "<http://blogs.msdn.com/b/usisvde/archive/2010/04/24/microsoft-offers-political-townhall-software-for-windows-azure.aspx>".

5 20dc.com (2010, 24 April). http://www.20dc.com/

CHAPTER 10

Engaging the Media

S INCE THE TIME OF JULIUS Caesar, political campaigns have needed to establish and protect their presence within public channels of information. Twenty centuries after Caesar's infamous and final sound bite, "Et tu, Brute," public information had become a technological force and the industry known as "the media," the fourth estate, the enemy of every person running for everything from the school board to the White House. "For a politician to complain about the press is like a ship's captain complaining about the sea," said British Member of Parliament and cabinet member Enoch Powell, a man who was no stranger to generating negative headlines.[1]

Gulf Coast Benefit

In addition to the candidates themselves, social media is a powerhouse for garnering support for specific causes, many of which become part of a candidate's core platform messaging. These local causes can become important positioning strategies for candidates. One example of how social media can rally people behind a cause was a Gulf Coast oil spill benefit event.

On July 1, 2010, the *Gulf Coast Benefit*, a group of 60 music venues, united nationwide to perform a series of concerts to benefit those directly impacted by the Gulf Coast Oil Spill and by utilizing social media set about to raise $100,000. Monies from the effort were channeled through *What Gives!?* to the *Gulf Restoration Network's* community based Gulf Future Campaign.

Local marketing was handled by independent club owners, but social media orchestrated the effort, which was organized and marketed in less than one month. Social media was utilized for the national tie to primary events and more than 65 locally organized awareness events.

"I have always believed that our online interactions are meant to facilitate our offline experiences and the *Gulf Coast Benefit* is a perfect example of that," said Sloane Berrent, co-producer of the affair. "You can find an event or make a donation online and we are using social media tools to bring people together.

"It's a way of extending the conversation that wasn't available even three years ago and it's a game changer."

Facebook, Twitter, Google, and PayPal were utilized. Also, by using the PopRule platform, mobile phones (Android and iPhone), as well as mobile users of MySpace, were utilized.

The central social media hub served two purposes: Getting people to attend a local event or donating.

Coast to coast social media on one site resulted in monies being raised toward helping people and wildlife during the world's worst environmental disaster.

Livingston, Geoff. "How the Gulf Coast Benefit is Using Social Media to Rally Support." Mashable.com. http://mashable.com/2010/07/01/how-the-gulf-coast-benefit-is-using-social-media-to-rally-support. July 1, 2010. http://www.gulfcoastbenefit.com/

We are well into the Web 2.0 era of shareable, interactive, all-the-time content. Per the buzz and punditry circulating within social media itself, user-generated content is ascendant and mainstream media is on the ropes. In the 21st century, no politician will have to utter a version of "you won't have Nixon to kick around anymore" since campaigns can essentially bypass the press corps and take their message straight to the people.

That said, don't plan a combined media wake and election victory party just yet. While mainstream media no longer comprises an information oligopoly, the coverage and opinions it distributes are still indispensible to political campaigns. And social media is not replacing the mainstream variety; the two are morphing into a new collective.

A study by Chitika Research[2] determined that "news" is the most popular content category for outbound traffic from Twitter and Facebook. Translation: people are spending much of their time sharing and seeking news on these hottest of social media sites. Further translation: good, old-fashioned journalism is the frequent basis of the most coveted kind of social media content, the kind that generates a click to a new destination on the Web.

Social media cannot be divorced from mainstream media or from a political campaign's overall media relations strategy (yet another reason not to dump social media on "the intern" and call it a day.) As it is redefining the news business, it is redefining the techniques of obtaining favorable coverage. For today's political campaigns, working with the media requires understanding social media and using it as a reference source, a direct communications tool, and a mutual platform with journalists.

Within a social media-driven media relations program, you must:

- Accommodate journalists' use of social media to search out stories
- Maintain a social media dialogue with journalists for pitching, commentary and rebuttal
- Pitch bloggers in ways that recognize how they emulate and differ from mainstream media journalists
- Monitor social media in determining new messages and pitches

- Issue social media releases in conjunction with standard releases
- Use social media sites for announcements, in conjunction with or in lieu of standard releases
- Build a Web 2.0 media room
- Cultivate user-generated content that mainstream media can incorporate into their own content
- Integrate social media into the crisis communications process
- Know when to take it offline in the times that social media is not the right tool for media relations

New Means to Traditional Ends

The intertwining of social media and mainstream media begins with how journalists are employing social media in their work. Studies reveal increasing numbers of media professionals use social media and web resources to research stories, obtain news angles and sources, and follow subjects of interest:

- Nearly 70 percent of journalists are using social networking sites, a 28 percent increase over the previous year (Second Annual Middleberg/SNCR Survey of Media in the Wired World).
- Over 73 percent of journalists read blogs to stay current on information pertaining to their beats (Bulldog Reporter and TEKGROUP International's 2010 Journalist Survey on Media Relations Practices).

- 73.4 percent use Facebook to research stories, and 55.5 percent use Twitter (2010 Journalist Survey on Media Relations Practices).
- 54.3 percent seek audio and video content from corporate websites (2010 Journalist Survey on Media Relations Practices).

"Increasingly, everyone in the business has to use social media," confirms Janet Kornblum, award-winning freelance writer and journalist who specialized in technology and culture as a staff writer for *USA Today* and CNET News. "You have limited time as a journalist."

A campaign's social media outreach must be designed with media relations in mind. Journalists will be accessing the same resources as voters to learn about the campaign, its accomplishments and its take on the issues. Fortunately, journalists can draw inspiration from information directed toward the public.

Advice for candidates includes offering interesting content within the Twitter feed, including useful information about positions held, campaign events, and so forth. Content should be authentic, substantive, and consistent, which demonstrates to journalists that you are a good source.

Campaigns should research key journalists' social media presence with tools like MuckRack.com, a Twitter directory for journalists that allows users to find media professionals by Twitter address, beat, and geographic location.

"In addition to these tools being valuable for learning about coverage and writing styles, it allows the communication director to build a rapport with journalists," says Alleigh Marré, a

Boston-based PR professional, political social media strategist, and Gov2.0 blogger.

Using social media to communicate directly with journalists and track their actions is similar to its use in other relationships. Following journalists on Twitter, friending them on Facebook, and connecting with them on LinkedIn are all acceptable practices. They should return the favor as it will help them cover their political and government beats. Like other social media associations, do not abuse the conduit with excessive or hostile communications.

Pay attention to what journalists are saying in their general social media posts. If they are looking for information or quotes on a particular subject, they are likely to announce it through social media. Respond quickly to such requests by offering background information, interview subjects, and relevant, user-generated content such as photos and video. If they contact you through a direct Twitter, Facebook, or LinkedIn message, respond as soon as possible.

Social bookmarking is another platform with media relations value. Sites such as delicious.com and Diigo.com allow users to create archives of web content. A campaign can curate an online library of third-party articles, studies, videos, and charts that support the candidate's positions and reinforce his or her suitability for the office. Users can network within social bookmarking sites and share information, creating another chance to connect with journalists and make their jobs easier by providing background material.

Blogger Relations

Blogs are a cornerstone of social media, representing one of the earliest and most visible forms of user-generated content. It is difficult to overstate blogs' influence on politics as a 24/7 outlet for independent commentary, a repeater station for mainstream media coverage, and a digital rally hall for volunteers and donors. Political campaigns may feel social media has suddenly descended upon them, but blogs have been a crucial part of communications strategy for years. As far back as December 2003, an article from Associated Press describes the presidential campaign of Gen. Wesley Clark enlisting the talents of blogging pioneer Cameron Barrett to combat "Internet-powered front runner Howard Dean."

Political blogs rank high in popularity among blogs of all categories. At the time of this writing, *The Huffington Post* was number one on Technorati.com's daily Top 100 blog list. *The Daily Beast* (with its frequently cited political channel), *Hot Air, Think Progress, CNN Political Ticker, Politics Daily, Mediaite, The Daily Dish*, and *Michelle Malkin* round out the first quartile. While the biggest political blogs are now media institutions, it is important to remember that new blogs can arise literally overnight to affect a race, particularly at the local and regional level. Every blog must be considered through the same set of media relations rules, a protocol unique to bloggers that accommodates both their similarities and differences when compared to traditional journalists.

Deciding which blogs matter can be accomplished through a combination of basic observations and more sophisticated measurements. In smaller races, blogs will reveal their relevance simply by commenting on the candidates and issues. Such blogs may be affiliated with local, traditional media and thus, immediately identifiable. Others can be located using a Google Blogs search of keywords, such as candidates' names. For larger races, blogs can be prioritized by their web metrics for traffic and/or influence as measured by sites such as Alexa, Technorati, and BlogPulse.com.

Blogging experts such as Jason Vines, author of the blog *Social Media Explorer*, and Deirdre Breakenridge, principal of Mango! Marketing, recommend immersion in blogs of consequence. Follow them. Read past posts. Begin commenting on posts. Responses from the campaign manager or the actual candidate will show the blogger and the blog's followers that you are paying attention and find the blog important, even if it is at odds with the candidate. This also puts your campaign into the dialogue, which is the essence of every influential blog. There is no guarantee that comments from the campaign will be made public, but an astute blogger will not filter them.

Direct contact with bloggers can occur through a number of means. Media database services such as Cision will have contact information for more prominent bloggers and mainstream media journalists who blog. Many blogs will have an email link to the blogger or a contact form on the "about" page.

Campaigns can also follow bloggers on Twitter and send them direct messages when they in turn follow the campaign. Pithy and personalized communications tend to rule in the blogosphere. Social media consultant and author Tamar Weinberg warns against using standard press releases in reaching out to bloggers. In-depth information should be held in reserve until after a blogger responds to a short pitch.[3]

Knowing a blog's tone and prior content will dictate pitches and follow-ups. Supportive blogs can receive more frequent and detailed information with greater likelihood that it will be used for content. Examine such blogs' readership and image. A blog that supports your candidate but spews invective and makes wild charges about your opponent can hurt your campaign's image. Choose your friends in the blogosphere fairly but wisely.

Care should also be taken when sending written pitches. Darren Rowse, founder of Problogger.net, warns that any information sent may end up verbatim in a post due to the Web's copy-and-paste culture and a freewheeling spirit among certain bloggers.

Blogs can be potent channels for exclusive information. Special interviews with the candidate or major announcements delivered through carefully chosen blogs can reach constituents quickly and spark more mainstream media coverage as they vie to break the news to their audiences.

"Bloggers are generally much more accessible, much more willing to write," says Adam Haverstock, communications consultant for Rincon Strategies, a marketing and community outreach firm that serves political campaigns. When distributing campaign news, he often goes first to bloggers with the eventual goal of driving mainstream media coverage. "They'll write on it immediately; then it will come out in print."

Blogs can develop stories that are important to the campaign but receiving insufficient coverage in traditional outlets. Active political bloggers are eager for scoops to burnish their newsmaker credentials. As an example, multiple blogs undermined the authenticity of documents used in a 2004 CBS News report as evidence of George W. Bush's dereliction of duty while in the National Guard.

Blogs also present more than the written word. Multimedia content such as web video and podcasts should be pushed to blogs or developed in cooperation with bloggers (see "User-Generated Content" later in this chapter).

Monitoring Social Media

Every social media program requires a monitoring strategy. It is the Web 2.0 equivalent of the polling and focus groups that political campaigns have used for decades. Social media monitoring directly affects campaign media relations by gauging:

- The most frequently discussed topics relating to the race, allowing the campaign to tailor media pitches and public communications accordingly
- The most frequently shared news stories, allowing the campaign to focus on the journalists and outlets exerting the most influence among people discussing the race via social media

Social media monitoring is easily accomplished—perhaps too easily as there are a large number of tools, platforms and sites that can track the online conversation. Allocation of resources and focus on essential outcomes are core to your success.

With more than 100 social media monitoring tools (and growing) it's prudent to clearly define your campaign goals and define that you really need these tools to measure.

Like popular social media platforms themselves, many social media monitoring tools are free. Google's "Updates" search (found under the "more" tab on the Google search bar) monitors Twitter mentions of search terms with a graph for mention frequency and the ability to track past occurrences of the term. The self-explanatory Twitter Search and Facebook Search plumb those respective platforms.

Twitter has its own search engine, www.search.twitter.com, which can send notices of keyword occurrences through an RSS feed. The Google Blogs search function reveals keywords occurring within individual blogs as do blog search engines such as Technorati and BlogPulse.com. Google Alerts can send notices of keyword appearances in blogs as can RSS feeds from sites such as Technorati.

Paid services can provide more sophisticated social media monitoring. Trackur.com allows users to follow many different social media channels and view results in a unified format. It can determine the influence of specific posts and content by measuring incoming links and traffic. Radian6 tracks a vast array of social media, providing analytics on traffic and influence. Pricing for such services can range from approximately $20 per month for Trackur's basic service to $500 per month for Radian6's entry point. A campaign's size and budget will quickly determine whether it should go the free or paid route with social media monitoring.

Social media monitoring to support media relations parallels a campaign's overall tracking of channels and sites. The methodology is similar to search engine optimization (SEO) techniques to gather paid search and organic search results. It comes down to keywords: candidates' names, issues, taglines, and geography (such as district or municipality). Qualities (e.g., "tax fighter," "weak on crime") can also be part of the search matrix if the terms are hot buttons. Specific headlines, journalists and outlets should also be part of the ongoing search to measure their popularity and influence. Maintain a spreadsheet to track keyword occurrence, organized by trends and topics. Many paid monitoring services will automate such reports.

The campaign team will want to develop a model of measurement that guides the timing and action taken from social media trends including frequency, sentiment, popularity, influence of followers, and more.

Social media monitoring results should guide media pitches and releases. Upon recognizing a positive trend for the candidate, the campaign can recommend new stories to substantiate it. Negative trends can be fought through the same methods. Determining the popularity of specific news features focuses a campaign on journalists and outlets wielding the most influence. This can be done by tracking social media mentions and links and by checking the popularity measurements for stories ("most read," "most shared," "most liked") found on media websites.

"We always seek out authors of pieces getting a lot of play," says Rachel Dodsworth, principal of Adsworth Media and social media specialist for 2010 gubernatorial and U.S. Senate races in Colorado. "We make sure to continuously push articles from the local media in order to further build relationships. At the same time, we ensure that our followers and supporters on Twitter are followed back. Users really enjoy the fact that a major candidate is following their tweets. To further solidify this relationship and ensure these users share the campaign's word as much as their own, we ensure to thank users for every retweet and post showing support."

Through this program of media monitoring and supporter connection, Dodsworth guides supporters to retweet and share positive stories, ultimately encouraging the journalists and outlets responsible to produce similar coverage to maintain traffic and readership. This is not an effort to slant journalism; it is a means to reinforce public response to certain types of coverage. In short, the media wants to produce stories that interest the public.

"Finding the hot button issue that can get your base excited is definitely key. Being on top of memes can get you a lot of online attention," says Adam Mordecai, a veteran of Howard Dean's campaign for president and partner/strategist at Advomatic, a web development and strategic planning firm. "What matters most, however, is a good sense of theatre, and a willingness to try something different that the journos haven't seen before. This is something we learned on the Dean campaign. Focusing that message on the personal rather than broad facts will help get people further engaged."

Releasing the News

Though it may seem as though every candidate who tossed his or her hat into the ring for the 2012 presidential elections did so via a handy tweet, the need for solid media channels remains important for any campaign's success.

The Social Media Release

Releasing the news in the social media era requires a blend of new and old methods, beginning with a Web 2.0 version of a PR staple. The social media release (SMR) is an evolved form of the standard press release, incorporating the tools and the tone of Web 2.0. Todd Defren, principal of Shift Communications, is credited with creating the first template for the social media release in 2006.

The social media release differs from a standard release through its brevity, sharable nature, and links to supporting online content—all hallmarks of social media itself.

Per the Defren template, which has been modified since its inception and is being continually adapted by its users, the social media release reduces verbiage while emphasizing the means to share its information and to view related content. It is placed on the Web with a unique URL and "distributed" though its links and sharing tools, not by a wire service or e-blast. Contact information and a headline comprise the beginning of the release. Beneath the headline, a bulleted list of facts can suffice for the copy.

The social media release links to a social bookmarking page. A political campaign can use this feature to juxtapose the release with independent articles and commentary that validate the candidate's relevant positions and actions.

Quotes are broken out in a separate section apart from the main copy. Defren recommends up to two quotes per individual with additional quotes available for outlets seeking exclusive information. Per the push for authenticity in social media, keep the quotes short and free of jargon and slogans.

The left sidebar of the social media release presents links to supporting multimedia content: images, podcasts/MP3 files, and video. The right sidebar contains moderated comments regarding the release and a blogroll of sites that link to the candidate's news. These last two elements embody social media's mandate for dialogue and transparency. They may seem edgy to many candidates and an invitation for negative remarks. Properly managed, comments and blogger links will show the candidate's connectedness and willingness to publicly back his/her positions. This openness and courage of conviction will not be lost on perceptive journalists.

The footer of the social media release contains sharing tools such as an RSS feed, a "Share This" universal bookmark widget, and tags for Technorati. These tools make it easier for journalists to find and follow the campaign's releases. The general public can benefit as well from such social media accessibility. Per social media experts such as David Meerman Scott, Brian Solis and Deirdre Breakenridge, releases are no longer just for the media; they are communications for all publics.

The Standard Press Release
The standard press release is not "dead," as is often speculated. It should be written with the concise sensibilities of Web 2.0—no rambling, posturing or stilted quotes. A traditional release is a good vehicle for a more "narrative" approach to the main copy, written

in a customary article style. It is also the center of the classic "push" strategy of media relations, sending information to the media via the wire or e-mail. A standard release should have a link to a corresponding social media release. This "doubling up" is perfectly acceptable as making information available through multiple channels has always been a sound media relations strategy.

Be sensitive to the preferred contact methods of journalists covering smaller-scale races. You may be waging a campaign in an area where political coverage is in the hands of an exclusive group of writers and editors who insist on more traditional forms of communication.

Jeff Gorell, 2010 candidate for California's 37th state assembly district and former aide and speechwriter to Gov. Pete Wilson, was facing a potential opponent who announced his exploratory committee exclusively on Facebook. Days passed and there was no local newspaper coverage of the announcement. Gorell asked the paper's political writer about the absence of the story, to which the writer responded: "I'm not going to start covering him unless he starts to act like a credible candidate and communicate with the media directly or with a press release."

Social Media Posts

Organizations commonly use Facebook, Twitter and other social media platforms to post news and announcements. Political campaigns should use this basic tactic as well. The intent is to increase opportunities to capture key audiences' attention quickly, give them the equivalent of a sound bite via the post (this premise is built into Twitter's character limit), and link them to more detailed information. Using social media to push releases and announcements simultaneously notifies journalists and the public. If an item is truly newsworthy, the media knows that word is out, compelling the members of the media to generate in-depth coverage and provide value to an aware audience.

Social media news posts can enhance the campaign's website, driving traffic to the site and help keep its content fresh.

"When I make a tweet, it will stream it onto the front of my website," says Jeff Gorell. "So it's an easy way for me to add content to my website when my IT guy can't put it up for a couple of hours."

Posting to social media sites can eliminate the need for many typical releases, namely those that call attention to positive media coverage or favorable poll results. A quick tweet or Facebook message directing viewers to the source content saves the effort and potential message dilution of a release to note a campaign "win."

Today's campaign doesn't necessarily need to write a press release if the media is telling the story they want. This frees a campaign to offer value-adds and issues-based stories that would enhance the stories that are already out there and working on behalf of the candidate.

The Web 2.0 Media Room

An online media room has been a communications requirement since the 1990s. A Web 2.0 media room enhances the concept using social media techniques, allowing journalists to access information more consistently and efficiently. Todd Defren, originator of the social media release, is also the early proponent of the Web 2.0 media room, introducing a template on his blog in 2007.

Defren and Lee Odden, founder of TopRank Online Marketing, both encourage the use of blog software and typical blogsite features in constructing a Web 2.0 media room. Odden cites blog software's content management capabilities, SEO enhancements, and automatic RSS features as the means to make an online media room's content simpler to locate within the site and easier to find when conducting web searches.

Defren uses blogsite structure liberally in his social media newsroom template, which like his social media release template is crowdsourced (a design derived from others' feedback and experiences) and opensourced (given freely to the online world in hopes the concept will spread).

In adapting Defren's corporate-oriented template to political campaigns, the upper left-hand corner contains the candidate's basic information including a link to his/her LinkedIn profile. Links and contact information for campaign media contacts occupies the top right-hand corner. A search window prominently displayed at the top of the page will allow journalists and other viewers to find content by keyword.

Archives for media coverage and news releases dominate the center of the newsroom page. Each post features an abstract and a link to the complete piece along with sharing tools for emailing and social bookmarking. Both the media coverage and news release sections allow visitors to opt for updates by RSS feed or e-mail.

The schedule section occupies the bottom center of the page. Social media tools can be used to document "time and place" for the candidate. Alleigh Marré recommends the use of Foursquare to display a candidate's whereabouts, whether you are planning a rally, an interview, or lunch at a local diner (note: updates are voluntarily entered). Foursquare posts can be synched to Twitter and Facebook, allowing the media and the public to track the candidate easily.

Defren's template also includes a multimedia gallery with links to images and videos, a social bookmarking section, and a tag cloud. This last component allows visitors to search for content by keyword with the most commonly occurring terms appearing in larger font to indicate their frequency and importance. The "blog-like" feature helps the members of the media to determine at a glance which topics are emphasized in the candidate's content.

Use of blog software can also be a budget saver for smaller campaigns, with many free or inexpensive products available. Eric Anderson, principal of SE2, a Colorado-based mass communications firm, points out that races for regional or local offices attract a limited number of interested media outlets. Campaigns must spend time and money accordingly in deploying their online media rooms.

New Media Considerations

User-Generated Content. Social media is user-generated content—written word, audio, photos, video, multimedia. Political campaigns spawn copious amounts, and mainstream media is increasingly embracing it both as a source of story leads and as content directly presented to its audiences per CNN.com's iReport.

"You definitely want to create as much user-generated content as possible," recommends Adam Haverstock. "It helps the media realize the campaign is larger than just the candidate."

A campaign should post basic guidelines on creating and presenting user-generated content, including tips on:

- Writing blog posts and social news articles including tone, length and how to develop a topic.
- Videography and photography including subject selection, basic composition and easy lighting techniques.
- Recording podcasts including use of basic recording equipment (most laptops have built-in microphones), writing scripts and conducting interviews.

- Uploading finished content to the campaign's channels and pages on sites like YouTube, Flickr and MyPodcast.com.
- Sharing finished content using social media sites.

Keep the advice simple and fun. Remind supporters that the campaign doesn't want slick or canned materials, that authenticity and "the voters' voice" are the most important aspects. Helping supporters create user-generated content is the Web 2.0 version of guiding them in writing letters to the editor (still an important function itself).

"Constituents who are incredibly passionate about your message will create an amazing piece of content that can help your campaign, however fanatical opponents will do the same," says Alleigh Marré, a Boston-based PR professional, political social media strategist, and Gov2.0 blogger. "It is important to find the 'safe' balance of listening to your audience, and still maintaining the integrity of your message."

Pitching journalists on user-generated content requires tact. "Let things be organic," says Janet Kornblum. "It's fine to start a conversation and then suggest that journalists check something out, but expect that if they find anything quotable or interesting they may want to contact the person who said it."

Social Media and Crisis Communications. Every political campaign must function as if it is in crisis mode even if nothing bad is happening. Social media provides a new opportunity to anticipate and counteract crises, but it must be used judiciously and integrated with overall communications strategy.

Brian Solis blogs that the social web has transformed crisis communications from a reactive discipline to a proactive one of "listening, observing and participating." Jeff Gorell confirms that he uses social media "as an early warning system on information, misinformation, and major movements of opponents."13 During the 2010 primary season, the sudden departure of a group of fans from his campaign's Facebook page—a particular bloc of people known for their ideological stance—alerted him to the entrance of a challenger for his party's nomination, giving him time to prepare new strategy and messaging.

Social media serves as an intelligence gatherer because it is where people learn about and share negative news, be it media coverage or user-generated content such as the 2006 video that derailed Sen. George Allen's campaign when he used the name "macaca" for an Indian-American videographer working for his opponent Jim Webb. According a *Washington Post* story, Allen's campaign manager dismissed the incident at the time. It has been common practice for campaigns to deem negative stories unimportant to minimize their significance and project a confident image. Rachel Dodsworth advises against such an approach.

"You can't call something a non-issue and hope it goes away," she explains. "Social media will tell you if you have an issue or not."

While a crisis will doom complacency, it also is not an occasion for kneejerk reactions, which can be all-too-easily transmitted through social media. Eric Anderson says, "The most important thing is to get the response right the first time, even if that takes a little longer. It's very difficult to undo the damage caused by starting off on the wrong foot."

Social media must work in concert with other communication tools. Once the crisis response moves forward, it may be the first means of communications a campaign chooses, its very use conveying a subtext of immediacy, openness and technological savvy. When the time is right for that communications, one additional advantage of a social media response is the insertion of the candidate's message directly into the online dialogue, allowing it to be observed and shared straight from the source.

Scott McInnis' 2010 campaign for Colorado governor offers an example of the importance of stemming negative social media flow with social media counteraction that also triggers mainstream media coverage. During the week of July 12, 2010, the candidate acknowledged plagiarism regarding an essay on water rights and a bylined newspaper column, attributing the improper use of source material to researchers and staffers.

On July 14, speculation grew that McInnis was dropping out. Into the night, social media officer Rachel Dodsworth noted rumors accumulating on Twitter and other social media she was tracking. At 8:00 a.m. on July 15, she directed an intern to prepare a tweet to counter the rumors. At approximately 9:30 a.m., the candidate tweeted that he was "in it to win it." The media quickly reported the tweet.

"People are going to talk about political campaigns no matter what. This is why you must play an active part in these communications to keep your message and image both consistent and authentic," Dodsworth says.

Although known for immediacy and authenticity, social media can become a barrier against mainstream media—deliberately or inadvertently. In a crisis, the candidate cannot say his/her piece via social media and declare the matter closed. Any initial statements, from a tweet to a video address posted on YouTube, must be considered an invitation for journalists' follow-up. It is acceptable to counter negative issues in campaign-generated content, but be prepared to respond promptly to media inquiries and to take questions.

When to Take it Offline

While social media can greatly increase the effectiveness of media relations, it is not a blanket solution. There are times when you need to take a conversation with the media offline to effectively transmit certain information and nurture journalist relationships.

Exclusives that give one outlet a head start over others require a personal touch. Standard rules about awarding exclusives still apply:

- Is the recipient of the story the best communications channel for the campaign?
- Does the recipient warrant the special treatment?
- Will you irreparably harm relationships with other media over the favoritism?

Potentially negative or damaging information should also be addressed face-to-face. The sensitivity of such issues calls for direct communication, which will also allow both the campaign and media side to interpret intent and meaning, qualities than cannot be conveyed nearly as well in electronic communication, especially in the typical shorthand of social media.

Running disagreements with the media should not be played out in social media. A posted rebuttal to an unfavorable piece can dissolve into a tweet war or its equivalent on other platforms. It used to be said that it was unwise to pick a fight with someone who buys ink by the barrel, meaning traditional media always had the last word due to their resources and control of communication. It may be tempting to think that has changed with Web 2.0 now that everyone has the same number of pixels; however, user-generated venting will wound a campaign.

"I don't see the percentage in engaging in a heated social media exchange," Eric Anderson says. "It just promotes the idea that this is a blood sport primarily serving as entertainment. I'd prefer to focus on getting my messages out without giving a platform to opposing views."

The signature issue of authenticity can dictate when social media is not the solution. "I don't like the idea of credible news sources quoting Twitter or Facebook without fact checking," says Adam Haverstock. "How many accounts get hacked every day?"

In the end, there is no program or web dashboard to tell you when to step away from social media and engage in a direct conversation. There are only the instincts and experience borne of able political campaign management.

As a longtime professional observer and practitioner of social media, Deirdre Breakenridge summarizes political campaigns' mandate to use it in their relationships with journalists.

Today, like-minded people come together in web communities. They decide how they want to share information, and, most of all, who they choose as their most trusted media sources. Traditional journalists realize this, as they create blogs and participate more in social networks. If political campaigns want to get the word out and connect directly to garner support, then they need to be where the people are congregating too. Social media truly takes the saying "government for the people by the people" to a whole new level.

Social media is not a goal unto itself. It is not a magical replacement for the traditional, independent public channels of information that have exalted and damned political campaigns, sometimes within the same news cycle. As it is for other crucial actions—organizing volunteers, raising funds, and getting out the vote—social media is a tool for working with the mainstream media. Successful campaigns will seize this important opportunity for engagement.

1 Powell, E. Retrieved 10 May 2010. http://www.searchquotes.com/Enoch_Powell_/Media/quotes/

2 Ruby, D. (2010, March 19). Twitter and Facebook are for News; MySpace is for Leisure. Chikita Insights. http://insights.chitika.com/2010/twitter-and-facebook-are-for-news-myspace-is-for-leisure/

3 Weinberg, T. (2009). *The New Community Rules: Marketing on the Social Web*. CA: O'Reilly Media, Inc.

CHAPTER 11

Iterative Campaigning

S OCIAL MEDIA IS SUCH A game-changer in politics because the once passive voters become active participants in a campaign. In addition to attending a rally, townhall, fundraising event, or a debate, the average citizen can now co-create the political dialogue with the use of online social networking tools, such as Facebook, Twitter, the blogosphere, Google, and YouTube.

Effective use of social media is a necessity for any campaign and will continue to be, just as email and a website were 10 years ago. The success of the Obama campaign during the 2008 presidential elections proved that strategic use of online social media, if leveraged effectively, opens up new avenues for communications and fundraising at little or no cost, allowing candidates to reach out to a larger audience for public campaign contributions, engage the public around campaign activities and recruit volunteers.

As more Americans from all age groups become regular users of the wide variety of online social media, candidates at the local, state and federal level are using online measures to garner offline support at rallies, townhalls and volunteer events, raise funds, and engage in discussion. Campaign messaging can now be a real-time 24-hour experience between a campaign and voting base. Online campaigning allowed Rep. Ron Paul (R-TX) to raise $6 million in one day from online donors through his website that solicited pledges for contributions to be made directly to the Paul campaign on the 234th anniversary of the Boston Tea Party — a technique that became known as a "money bomb."

Yet, while social media provides a new construct for engagement, it does not replace the need for offline communication, such as canvassing door-to-door through neighborhoods, talking with potential supporters through rallies or townhall meetings, holding fundraising events to excite supporters, or producing carefully crafted campaign television ads.

According to a Pew Internet and American Life Project survey, "despite the growth of the Internet for campaign news, television remains the public's main source for such information," even though 15 percent of all American adults reported they got most of their campaign news during the election from the Internet, up from 7 percent in the mid-term election of 2002.[1] Given that young adults are overwhelmingly more frequent users of the Internet and older citizens still prefer to acquire their information via traditional media, to engage all voting age constituents, political campaigns now have the opportunity and the obligation to reach their voting base through both mediums, one reinforcing the other.

Candidates can reap the most benefits by producing a campaign ad meant for television or recording a video of the candidate's latest speech to a townhall meeting and posting it on YouTube, then writing a Twitter or Facebook update alerting fans and followers of the video link. This link can also inform supporters of the date and time the ad will be airing on television or when the next townhall meeting will be so supporters can tune in for more.

Online and offline elements must work in unison. Therefore, this section highlights ways in which political campaigns can and should use online measures for garnering this offline support using examples from campaigns across the United States. Moreover, while utilizing social networking sites can bring many benefits, social media sites, such as YouTube, Twitter, and Facebook have also posed challenges to the ability to which campaign staffers can control the image and message of the candidate. Therefore, this section will also discuss pitfalls to avoid, or risk losing out on vital campaign contributions, not to mention growing and mobilizing a strong base of support.

Finally, "the future of elected government" may soon be "measured in fans and followers, as well as votes," observes one expert in social media.[2] Those fans file petitions. This issue alone—filing the online petition - is essential to understanding elections in the social media age.

Strategy Recap

The Obama campaign website, "Organizing for America," was, as we recall, a social networking tool unto itself. They used a program called MyBO, developed by Facebook co-founder Chris Hughes. That allowed them to locate local events to support Obama's candidacy, such as rallies, fundraisers and canvassing. On it, each supporter could create a unique own profile, including the ability for the user to maintain a blog and create a short profile and track fellow local and national supporters' activities and campaign efforts on the "Activity index. Ultimately, using this online platform, the Obama campaign focused on "hyperlocal approach," encouraging individual-to-individual connections using online social tools to invigorate its core on the local level.[3]   Today, of course, hyperlocal is embedded in much digital journalism. The merger of AOL and Huffington Post has resulted in a pool of thousands of reporters able to cover small patches such as Darien, Connecticut.

Not So Social Across the Pond?

On May 6, 2010, the United Kingdom general election was held and unlike Barack Obama's presidential campaign, a limited amount of social media was utilized to elect Conservative leader David Cameron, Labour leader Gordon Brown, and Liberal Democrat leader Nick Clegg to the House of Commons. Since none of the parties achieved the 326 seats needed for an overall majority, a hung parliament resulted, wherein no party was able to command a majority in the House of Commons.

The Conservatives and the Liberal Democrats talked for five days, and there was an aborted attempt to put together a Labour/Liberal Democrat coalition. But on May 11, Gordon Brown announced his resignation as Prime Minister, ending 13 years of Labour government. Queen Elizabeth II accepted the resignation and invited Conservative David Cameron to form a government and become Prime Minister. On May 12, the Liberal Democrats emerged from a meeting of their Parliamentary party and Federal Executive to announce that the coalition deal had been approved, sealing a stable coalition government of Conservatives and Liberal Democrats.

During the campaign, the three main party leaders engaged in a series of televised debates, the first time ever in a British election. However, compared to the United States at that time, social media hadn't quite taken root. Historically, the British have not been known to spend money extensively online, let alone contribute money to political campaigns online, so the jury is still out on the future of digital campaigning. However, along with party political broadcasts, newspaper articles and direct mailings, some blogging, tweeting, online fundraising, and texting took place.

Sudhaman, Arun. "Election 2010: Parties turn to old-school campaigning tactics to woo voters." BRANDREPUBLIC. "<http://www.brandrepublic.com/News/Emaillt/1001159/ DA062C7573C52E3489613D083901. May 6, 2010.>"
"<http://web.ebscohost.com/ehost/pdfviewer?vid=6&hid=1128sid=40310e95-4238- 8055-3d9aec0. >"
"<http://en.wikipedia.org/w/index.php?title=United_Kingdom_general_election,_2010& printable=yes>".
"<http://www.reuters.com/article/idUSTRE6456NZ20100510>"

However, that's not a realistic model for most political campaigns, at least not yet. But it could be with the proliferation of mobile apps. Right now, not even the most well-funded Congressional campaign office can afford to maintain and manage such an elaborate hyperlocal system. Instead, campaigns are leveraging existing, broader social networking tools as essential and affordable means to connect with all the constituents in their districts.

As cited at the start of this book, Republican State Rep. Justin Amash, for example, was one of the first legislators to post all of his votes on the floor of the Michigan House of Representatives on Facebook. He then responds to and comments on fans' opinions of his votes.

Not only did posting his votes in real-time earn him a reputation for open social policies by the media, but he has since announced his candidacy for U.S. Congress on Facebook. He says, "Because I'm willing to explain myself and account for my actions, I've gained Facebook fans from across the political spectrum. Some of my best interactions are with people who disagree with my votes. I'm trying to foster the kind of civil, rational discourse that has been missing from politics for a long time."[4]

Furthermore, the service called Ning is also revolutionizing the ability to coalesce the many social networking platforms into one. Ning is a social platform that allows candidates to create their own social network and allows the campaign to connect with grass-roots supporters, with the ability to link the site to the candidate's Twitter and Facebook accounts. For example, the campaign staff of Sen. Scott Brown, who ran in 2010 to take Ted Kennedy's vacant Massachusetts Senate seat, created a Ning page called the "Brown Brigade," which allowed supporters to "hook up with people in a brigade in [their] area." According to Brown's social-media strategist, "The channel worked in all directions: Brown's staff could reach his supporters, his supporters could respond to him, and supporters could find one another to organize."[5]

Political campaigns can also learn from the social media strategies in 2010 by the Democratic and Republican parties. Despite Obama's appeal to the younger generation and his ability to leverage social media to engage voters, results have shown that the Republicans have far surpassed the Democrats in their ability inform citizens and encourage participation and debate.

As of September 23, 2010, Republican candidates for Senate had more than four times as many fans on Facebook: over 1.4 million compared with 300,000 for Democratic candidates.[6] Democratic candidates are maintaining their localized approach of canvassing and using social tools to make peer-to-peer connections. While it is difficult to tell if mobile tools will impact voting, perhaps the most exciting development for the Democrats is the party's use of mobile.

The Organizing for American (OFA) app allows party supporters to find people living in their region to canvas. The app also provides canvassing tips to OFA app users to make sure the ground-level work is effective. The Republicans are focusing on reaching out to the local core, then empowering the core to push out on a national and local level. Republicans are working on constructing a national community behind their campaign strategies by tapping into the influence of local bloggers to be the voice of the party. That in itself has been creating encouragement across the entire country for local races.[7]

Republican political outreach efforts are showing promise in the field. While voter turnout always drops in a midyear election, a CNN poll conducted in July 2010 showed that in this round of elections only 27 percent of Democrats were extremely or very enthusiastic about voting this year, compared with 42 percent of Republicans.[8] According to Shana Glickfield, co-founder of the BeeKeeper Group, a Washington, DC public affairs firm, "The Democrats seem to be sticking with the tactics that brought them into power, whereas the GOP, as the challenger, is exploring more innovative ways to tap the power of new media." She says, "Both are effective and embrace the strengths of technology and community, but I see the Republicans getting the added bonus of attracting blogger and mainstream media attention for innovating in the campaign space."[9]

Nicole Russo, Legislative Aide to New York State Senator Kemp Hannon, notes that her campaign's "goal by using social media is to have an active conversation with our constituents. Sometimes we have to ask the hard questions and get real, truthful, and sometimes harsh answers. The more we know about what our constituents are thinking, the better we can serve them." [10] One major best practice is for candidates or social media staffers to be accessible online at all times and to pinpoint their target audience.

Social media expert, Julielyn Gibbons, President of i3 Strategies, an online strategy consulting firm, and Senior Fellow at the New Organizing Institute in Washington, DC, teaches that the most successful use of social media is to have a "cyclical message strategy." She says, in her clients' sites every element is linked to all the other elements. For example, at the end of a YouTube video there's the URL for the website, Facebook page, and Twitter account. Actually, anyone online who doesn't have this integrated linking approach is wasting time. The first directive given the web developer is to ensure everything is linked together.

Your Toolkit

Keeping the idea of a cyclical messaging strategy in mind, the following further details best practices when using Twitter, Facebook, YouTube, and campaign websites to demonstrate how candidates have best leveraged social media to make real differences in their campaigns, online and offline.

Twitter. Twitter allows candidates to post short message bursts to announce events, links to blog posts, and breaking news. It allows a campaign to instantly send a succinct message to thousands of followers. The short length of the message allows other followers to re-post the message to their own followers so that a message can go viral within minutes. Senator Claire McCaskill, D-Mo., has been named in lists of the best Twitter-users in Congress because she intersperses her policy positions and Washington action with personal statements in her daily Twitter posts.

In addition frequently interspersing policy positions with personal thoughts, other best practices that will encourage followers to contribute funding, advertise events, or pass along the word. To monitor a candidate's message or feedback from followers, an excellent strategy is to frequently monitor the candidate's name on search.twitter.com to see how tweeters are commenting or responding.

Another critical tool is to promote an event, campaign, or relevant news with corresponding Twitter hashtags. Twitter hashtags help spread information on Twitter while also helping to organize the information. *Mashable*, the social media news blog, recommends using a hashtag when attempting to organize a large group, a great feature for organizing comments by supporters of a particular candidate or political party.

Mashable notes, "if everyone agrees to append a certain hashtag to tweets about a topic, it becomes easier to find that topic in search, and more likely the topic will appear in Twitter's Trending Topics." Campaigns can create their own hashtags or use services such as What the Trend?, Twubs, Hashtags.org, and Tagalus to find information on thousands of hashtags on popular topics being discussed on Twitter. A recent awareness campaign by the Republican National Committee demonstrates the potential success of using hashtags to organize and spread a message.

The awareness campaign hit the web with $16,000 behind it, and Republican influencers propelled the message to the fore of Twitter with a related hashtag. Links circled the blogosphere through the deployment of more than 22,000 widgets. The effort leaked onto Facebook and turned into a fundraiser, eventually netting about $1.6 million, including eight online donations of $16,200 a piece.[11]

Moreover, another great service can help to track a candidate's history of messaging on Twitter, Twapperkeeper.com allows a user to save his Twitter posts allowing the campaign to assure they are maintaining a consistent political message. To further develop and promote a positive image, candidates can use Twitter's photo-sharing site called Twitpic, where candidates can share their photos campaigning on the road.

While more established politicians feel the need to maintain a carefully controlled message to avoid controversy, another strategy, often used by the underdogs or challenger candidates, is the "attack tweet."

These candidates often have little to lose and "can do things that established political figures can't do and wouldn't dare do," says Ronn Torossian, CEO of 5W PR, a New York-based public relations firm. He remarks, "the outsider can shoot from the hip." Mimicking the traditional opponent disparaging through television campaign ads, the "2010 tweet is a far cry from the polite Twitter dispatches of 2008.. In 2010, these messages "are scrappier and more emotional than the kinds sent out in 2008," says David Gudelunas, associate professor of communication at Fairfield University in Connecticut. "Those first tweets two years ago were largely 'antiseptic,'" he says, "dispensing details of campaign appearances and urging followers to vote."[12]

While the "attack tweet" can be controversial or even inappropriate, relatively anonymous candidates are making news across the US, even though they often barely hold a campaign office or budget. In the Delaware Senate race between GOP Rep. Mike Castle and Tea Party-affiliated Christine O'Donnell, O'Donnell's campaign tweets to followers were laced with controversial personal comments. Comments included complaints that she was being picked on because she's a conservative woman.

Facebook. Facebook not only allows candidates to post pictures, add videos, send detailed mass messages, but it invites political candidates to have conversations with their fans. This personal feedback engages the fan on a personal level, so much so that a 2008 analysis of candidates' uses of Facebook in the 2006 midterm election showed "that the majority of people who write on candidate walls perceive that they have fairly close relationships with these politicians. While there is not a great deal of self disclosure about issues or personalities, most commenters see themselves as friends of the candidates."[13] More importantly, Facebook facilitates dialogue between candidate and constituent. In a study examining 100 congressional Websites, Taylor and Kent (2004) found politicians' sites to be one-way communication channels void of reciprocal dialogue. By maintaining a frequently updated Facebook page, updating 'fans' on relevant rallies, policy issues updates, and news articles, supporters can react to these comments in real time. In return, supporters should expect a response from candidates, as a "candidate can ignore an email, but snubbing a "wall post" can be seen by the world."[14]

Some other best practices campaigns use to maintain their Facebook page include daily updates via wall posts to fans, timely responses to fan comments on the candidate's Facebook page, and frequently updated photos, event listings, or other information a fan may find interesting. For instance, New York State Senator Kemp Hannon's Facebook profile has become almost his personal news site. His constituents know what he's doing, both in the legislature and in his personal life.

Perhaps even more effective is to convince opponents of the candidate to fan the Facebook page. According to Josh Koster, Managing Partner of Chong + Koster, a digital consulting firm that works on political campaigns, "Why not 100 percent supporters? Because by leaving just a few haters on the page (and thus ensuring massive back-and-forths in the comments threads) we ensure higher marks from Facebook's Edge Rank algorithm." In addition, Koster notes the "importance of keeping 99% of the Page's discourse on your side to dominate the conversation, which may convince casual visitors of your point of view."[15]

Video. The most popular video-sharing website is YouTube. After Google and Facebook, YouTube was the third most visited website in the world as of June 2010. Posting campaign ads, videos of the candidate in action at rallies and events, or posting links to relevant videos, YouTube can bring multiple advantages to a political campaign. Other benefits emanate from setting up a YouTube channel. Montana Governor Brian Sweitzer was able to broadcast all of his campaign commercials to even the most sparsely populated areas of his state.

However, according to Ridout, Fowler, and Brandstetter, "[f]or television, simply having the set turned on is enough to guarantee exposure. The Internet requires the producer to prompt the user to choose to access the web, instead of television, choose to access YouTube, and finally choose to access a particular video. Prodding users to make those choices requires other resources." Campaigns must post links to these videos on multiple social networking accounts to guide more intentional viewership.

YouTube may also have indirect impacts, such as the ability to set the print media's agenda. Just as televised political ads are frequently covered in both newspapers and local news broadcasts, online advertising may be seen as newsworthy. One reason is because it is usually immediate and fresh. For instance, YouTube may help to put scandals on the agenda that may have gone unnoticed before the popularization of this site. In the 2006 mid-term elections, Republican Senator George Allen's chances at reelection in Virginia were seriously damaged by video spread widely on YouTube. During a campaign event speech,, as most of you remember, Allen referred to a student of Indian ancestry working for the opposing campaign as a "macaca," a derogatory term.

We all know the rest of that story. The video was then reported on the front page of *The Washington Post* and on cable and network television news shows. Senator Allen gave two public apologies, but was quickly no longer the leading contender for the 2008 Republican presidential nomination. His narrow loss of that election sent a message about how politics was a different game because of the Internet. The *New York Times* reported that Senator Joseph Lieberman lost to Ned Lamont in Connecticut's 2006 Democratic primary partly due to Lamont's use of YouTube. Lamont and pro-Lamont bloggers frequently posted flattering interviews of Lamont on YouTube and unflattering video of Senator Lieberman.[16]

To help monitor a candidate's image and message, while simultaneously encouraging supporters to connect on the same platform, YouTube has developed a new tool to help political candidates better deliver their messages to their audiences called the YouTube You Choose 2010 Campaign Toolkit.

Campaigns can apply to have their own YouTube Politician channel, a channel that "supports branding, longer videos, custom thumbnails, and includes Google Moderator and YouTube Insight for video analytics." By laying out some extra money, campaigns can "pay for the ability to add call-to-action overlays to videos, run their TV spots as in-stream ads in other YouTube videos and promote select videos as ads for search terms via Promoted Videos."[17]

Online Advertising. Online advertising is also becoming a bigger factor in the 2010 election season. Google has seen an increase of 800 percent of adoption rates of online advertising for gubernatorial and senatorial races since 2008.[18] Moreover, Google and Facebook are encouraging campaigns to integrate their online and offline outreach. That will have TV commercials sending the same messages as online ads and YouTube videos. Online advertising has proven to be a successful time investment for many candidates, not only because it is low-cost and targeted. A candidate can invest in a specific Facebook or Google ad that can be customized to appear for anyone who lives in his or her district and lists in their profile that they are interested in health care issues, for example. Virginia's U.S. Representative Frank Wolf (R-Dist. 10) used ads tied to Google search terms for the first time for his reelection campaign. The campaign to re-elect Virginia U.S. Rep. Gerald Connolly (D-Dist. 11) now includes Facebook ads this year.[19]

Candidates in the 2010 election cycle had also been taking advantage of Google's new service on YouTube that helps candidates further target voters. The service uses Google's in-stream ads, those brief commercials you see before YouTube clips to go after potential voters with "geo-location technology and content interest-targeting." According to Andrew Roos, Google's account executive for the election and issue ads team, "In stream ads are probably the hottest thing in political advertising right now. This was a product that wasn't available in the 2008 presidential campaign, and now we're seeing dozens of candidates using it in over 15 battleground states." For example, Mid-term senate candidates, such as Marco Rubio (FL) and Dino Rossi (WA), took advantage of Google by simply re-purposing television ads to run on YouTube.

Tom Barrett, when running for Governor of Wisconsin, was able to reach nearly 500,000 Wisconsin voters using in stream ads. Representative Michele Bachmann (R-MN) geo-targeted voters attending the state fair via their cell phones and Sen. Russ Feingold (D-WI) blanketed the Google Content Network in his state––a tactic he called the Cheddar Bomb. Since then, Bachmann has announced her presidential campaign.

Ultimately, candidates will still spend a large part of their campaign fund producing ads meant for television, but these ads can be re-used within many formats with traditional and online media outlets. Moreover, once the ads are online, the ads can be disseminated at no cost, simply through the work of supporters, bloggers, and tweeters.

Websites. There is a new "baseline" of online strategies for anyone seeking an elected office. Every candidate, whether local, state, or federal, has a website users can refer to. After reviewing the homepages of the candidates running for the gubernatorial elections being held in 37 states in 2010, OhMyGov, a political blog focusing on public sector innovations and advances, found that is an ideal template to the homepage.[20]

First, OhMyGov praised the presence of location maps, calendars and event listings that showed where candidates were appearing next on the campaign trail. These maps were more interactive than in previous years, allowing users to track where the candidate is, will be and has been. Second, nearly every candidate had an "issues" section. OhMyGov recommended the "issues" section to be structured with a brief overview of the candidate's stance for each larger issue, followed by a link leading to a longer essay on the subject or a PDF of a policy paper. Also important was displaying a widget with the numbers of the candidate's Facebook fans.

While not a regular feature on the websites reviewed, also recommended was displaying Facebook or Twitter update feeds on their homepage, as this indicates to one-time visitors the "like" rating for the candidate. Another common feature are video clips users can easily find and choose to play. OhMyGov also highly recommends "using the social media platforms as on-site frameworks for content rather than solely as foreign satellite web presences" and a section that calls for ideas from visitors of the site to further engage with constituents. For example, Rep. Peter Hoekstra's (R-MI) invited anyone to leave a comment on the "idea bus" on his homepage. Finally, donate and volunteer buttons were displayed prominently on the site to encourage visitors to provide support not only on the computer, but also through face-to-face support.[21]

The Online Petition

According to European political researcher Andranik Tumasjan, "previous research has shown that social media is widely used for political deliberation and that this deliberation reflects the political landscape of the offline world. The number of friends and followers can predict public opinion about a candidate. For instance, studies have found that a candidate's number of Facebook supporters can be a legitimate predictor of electoral success. In addition, Tumasjan found after analyzing over 100,000 Twitter messages mentioning parties or politicians prior to the 2009 German federal election that "Twitter can be considered a valid indicator of political opinion" and "closely corresponds to political programs, candidate profiles, and evidence from the media coverage of the campaign trail."[22]

Another way to gauge public sentiment is to analyze the number of signatures on an online petition. Online petitions have gained popularity among political social movements because it is much less expensive to create an online petition than it is to create and run an offline petition drive. On the site Act.ly (http://act.ly/petitions), online users can launch a petition through their Twitter account to reach the social media world. To show disapproval of a public policy or political event, government officials and American citizens, alike, are passing around online petitions, sending links to the petitions through mass emails and on their social networking sites.

For example, in February 2010, Senator Dick Durbin started an online petition called, "Fed Up with the Filibuster" to urge citizens to start discussing reforming the 60-vote requirement. In 2009, about 65,000 people signed an online petition protesting President Obama's scheduled May 17 commencement address at the University of Notre Dame, "saying the president's views on abortion and stem cell research 'directly contradict' Roman Catholic teachings." While the Notre Dame petition garnered much media attention and many signatures, the President spoke at Notre Dame on schedule.

To mobilize support, non-governmental organizations, such as MoveOn, often encourage users on their email lists to send pre-written letters by email to Members of Congress about their issue of grievance for their users to quickly copy and paste. These organizations hope that a Congressperson receiving hundreds of thousands of emails from constituents will demonstrate a public show of force around the issue.

Clay Shirky, an author who writes, teaches, and consults on social and economic effects of the Internet, writes that while previously the handwritten letter indicated that many voters in the district cared about a certain issue, "email is the wrong tool for lobbying Congress" because it "enormously lowers the transaction cost of sending a message while creating superdistribution...the cost of lobbying congress is so low that an e-mail message has become effectively meaningless." Public opinion, the number of pre-written emails sent to Congress, is falsely inflated by how effortless the act of forwarding an email is. Instead, Shirky recommends that every organization that lobbies Congress "would be better served by a less convenient, more expensive tool" to show true commitment.[23]

Allocation of Money for Online Social Media

The majority of money allocated to social media is now put towards online advertising. President Barack Obama spent 4 percent of his budget in his 2008 presidential campaign online. In 2004, the average online political ad spending for campaigns was 0.8 percent. Massachusetts Republican Scott Brown running to take Senator Ted Kennedy's empty seat, used Google ads, mobile applications and text messages to reel in voters to effectively defeat Martha Coakley. While one would expect campaigns to imitate the successful social media campaign strategies of Obama in 2008 and Sen. Scott Brown in 2010, only a handful of campaigns are putting large sums of money into expensive online advertising, such as banner ads.[24]

Campaigns are sticking to low-cost social media networking sites and keyword search features to harness the benefits of social media. According to Borrell & Associates, political spending on digital media should double this year vs. 2008, reaching $44.5 million. Overall, this is small, considering this allocation of money is estimated to be only one percent of total political media dollars.

Communications experts have found that candidates are still spending large sums of money on television advertising, which is estimated to raise two of every three dollars of political media budgets. That's primarily because in local elections TV advertising has a good track record for getting candidates elected. Candidates would rather spend on this proven method for advertising and use the Internet for its free communications platforms.

If candidates are going to allocate money on web advertising, Google search ads are one of the first places candidates are spending their money, with locally targeted Facebook self serve ads becoming a staple. Other newer online technologies being utilized are Google's "network blasts," which determine whether residents in the candidate's district or state view certain web pages, then places the candidate's ads to these relevant online users.

Facebook may be more effective when campaigns want to target ads to specific demographics. Adding Facebook "fan box widgets" on candidate websites can allow a person visiting the candidate's website to automatically become the candidate's fan on Facebook by clicking the widget. Moreover, candidates can now have ads appear on the homepage of all Facebook users in their state or district, regardless of whether the user is the candidate's fan.

Yet, once candidates successfully build an army of volunteers and supporters through this combination of online, print and television advertising, using these volunteers most effectively costs money. For instance, canvassers are issued handheld computers to log voters' responses as they go door to door and volunteers must be trained on paid individuals' time to make sure they're directed to the right places at the right time.

Moreover, even if a candidate decides to post all ads directly to YouTube, rather than pay for heavy production and air time for television spots, there are still the high hidden costs, such as for legal review.

Digital Pitfalls to Avoid in Political Campaigning

Public commenting on blogs and social networking sites and the ability to record videos at low cost then post them to the world causes challenges for the campaign to control the image and message of the candidate. Members of Congress were criticized in February 2010 for "tweeting" during President Obama's economic recovery speech after Joe Barton, Representative for the sixth district of Texas, posted, "Aggie basketball game is about to start on espn2 for those of you that aren't going to bother watching pelosi smirk for the next hour."

Moreover, adopting social media platforms is only successful if utilized effectively. Not keeping supporters engaged in the campaign is a worst practice. Responding to public comments posted on candidate blogs and Facebook pages allows the commenter to feel a personalized relationship, regardless of whether the comment supports or disapproves of the candidate. Howard Dean's 2006 campaign, for instance, did male digital communications available to his supporters but failed to involve them directly online. Such is an example of integrating a strategic communication tactic, but not exploiting it.

Even more disappointing is Barack Obama's Organizing for America in 2010. In 2008, the website encouraged 8 million volunteers to campaign on the streets for Obama. In 2010, there was only a tenth of the numbers from 2008. According to *TIME*, "neglect is to blame."[25]

In an op-ed in the *New York Times*, William Powers noted, "Twitter and Facebook aren't going to save the world. But when used alongside other tools of human connectedness—including some very old ones, like the face-to-face conversations, meetings and protests...the new technologies can be extremely useful." Ultimately, there is a baseline of social media tools a campaign must use to resonate with the voting base.[26]

Social media tools, such as Google and Facebook ads allow campaigns to target certain demographics and bring likeminded supporters together on one forum to engage in political discussion. Malcolm Gladwell in an interview in *The New Yorker* explains the gold standard of organizing through social media. He explains, "What Twitter and Facebook are capable of doing is introducing a very large group of people to a subject or an issue. The hard part is getting them to go beyond that introduction and dig in deeper— and that leap requires some additional form of social engagement. The Obama election campaign did a very good job of doing both—augmenting social media tools with old-school grass roots organizing. To me, that's the gold standard."

Yet, using these tools effectively does not guarantee physical presence at the voting booth, at political rallies, or dollars for the campaign fund. Evgeny Morozov, author of *The Net Delusion: The Dark Side of Internet Freedom*, reminds us that "we should not confuse mobilizing with organizing. The Internet excels at mobilizing people to rally behind political causes (obviously, not all of them democratic)—but someone still needs to engage in long-term strategic organization."

Traditional and new media must be intertwined. Obama's 2008 presidential campaign showed how the Internet facilitated a centralized campaign to behave in a decentralized manner. Given all the advantages of using social media to build a wide base of support, candidates are still traveling the country, state, and district to connect with their voting base in person.

At this point, online efforts are in addition to, not instead of, more traditional outreach efforts. Yet, there are ways to merge the two so that social media followers can still try to make it to the rally, or the fundraiser. Jeff Barnett, Democratic candidate for Virginia's 10th district, was traveling the district by foot to campaign to his voting base earlier in 2010. His supporters could follow his progress via Facebook, Twitter and online videos.

While social media allows challengers and first time candidates name recognition in a way that was not possible before, political campaigns, to be successful, must constantly be putting out new information. While it is easier to link one social network to the other though new online platforms mentioned above, an online presence is not enough. "You still have to be in the mail and on the phone. It's just another layer," said the communications director of the Barnett campaign.

Campaigns still send direct mail, call supporters, buy TV ads, knock on doors and meet with potential voters at community events. Although an online presence has become essential, pressing the flesh will always still count for a lot.

1 Pew Internet and American Life Project, (2008)
2 Silverman, M. (2010 June). How Political Campaigns Are Using Social Media for Real Results. *Mashable*. ",<http://mashable.com/2010/06/09/political-campaigns-social-media/>".
3 Livingston, G. (2010, September 24). Social Media: The New Battleground for Politics. *Mashable*. "<http://mashable.com/2010/09/23/congress-battle-social-media/#comments.>"
4 Silverman.
5 Yan, S. (2010, February 4) How Scott Brown's Social-Media Juggernaut Won Massachusetts. *TIME*. "<http://www.time.com/time/nation/article/0,8599,1960378,00.html.>"
6 Carr, A. (2010, September 23) Republicans Dominate Democrats in Social Media. *Fast Company*. "<http://www.fastcompany.com/1690878/republicans-dominating-democrats-in-social-media>".
7 Livingston.
8 Broom, J. (2010, August 28) Election 2010: Younger Voters Not So Eager This Time. *The Seattle Times*. "http://seattletimes.nwsource.com/html/localnews/2012750934_youngvoters29m.html."
9 Silverman.
10 Livingston.
11 Livingston.
12 Goodale, G. (2010, September 15) Potent tool for 'tea party' political campaigns: the 'attack tweet'. *The Christian Science Monitor*. "<http://www.csmonitor.com/USA/Election-2010/Vox-News/2010/0915/Potent-tool-for-tea-party-political-campaigns-the-attack-tweet.>"
13 Sweetser, K. D. & Weaver Lariscy, R. (2008). Candidates Make Good Friends: An Analysis of Candidates' Uses of Facebook. *International Journal of Strategic Communication*. 2(3), 175-198.
14 Hopper, R. (2010, January 18) Social Networking Becoming a Staple of Political Campaigns. *Associated Content*. "<http://www.associatedcontent.com/article/2603439/social_networking_becoming_a_staple_pg3.html?cat=15.>"
15 Silverman.
16 Lizza, R. (2006, August 20) The YouTube Election. *The New York Times*. http://www.nytimes.com/glogin?URI=http://www.nytimes.com/2006/08/20/weekinreview/20lizza.html&OQ=_rQ3-D1&OP=5d2c95d9Q2FQ3EdQ2AQ3EfbGcybbw7Q3E7JJiQ3EJYQ3E7JQ3EdQ2AQ2Ae5syQ2AP5Q2AdQ3E7JQ265Q51Q51XQ25FwQ5CQ26.
17 Van Grove, J. (2010, May) Google Launches New Tools for Political Campaigns. *Mashable*. "<http://mashable.com/2010/06/03/google-campaign-toolkits/.>"
18 Carr, A. (2010, August 23) Candidates Turn to YouTube for Geo-Specific Ad Campaigns for Mid-term Elections. *Fast Company*. "<http://www.fastcompany.com/1684457/google-you-tube-geo-specific-political-ads-mid-term-elections>"
19 Schumitz, K. (2010, September 22) Popularity of social media adds 'new layer' to political campaigns. *Fairfax Times*. "<http://www.fairfaxtimes.com/cms/story.php?id=2210.>"
20 Pinto, A. & Malseed, M. (2010, August 5) Trends in 2010 Campaign Web Sites: The Governors. *OhMyGov.com*. "<http://ohmygov.com/blogs/general_news/archive/2010/08/05/trends-in-2010-campaign-websites-the-governors.aspx>"
21 Pinto, Malseed.
22 Tumasjan, A. et al. (2010) Predicting Elections with Twitter: What 140 Characters Reveal about Political Sentiment. *Association for the Advancement of Artificial Intelligence*, 178-185.
23 Shirky, C. (2008) *Here Comes Everybody: The Power of Organizing without Organizations*. New York: The Penguin Group.
24 Hart, K. (2010, April 3) Google, Facebook prepare for political ad bonanza in midterm elections. *The Hill*. "<http://thehill.com/blogs/hillicon-valley/technology/90483-google-facebook-prepare-for-political-ad-bonanza-in-mid-term-elections.>"
25 Newton –Small, J; Time Magazine; 09 September, 2010.
26 Powers, W. (2010, September 30) Digital and Traditional Tools. *The New York Times*. "<http://www.nytimes.com/roomfordebate/2010/09/29/can-twitter-lead-people-to-the-streets/digital-and-traditional-tools-arent-mutually-exclusive>"

CHAPTER 12

After the Vote—What Happens Next?

WHILE POLITICAL CAMPAIGNS are employing social media efforts as part of their campaigning and fundraising strategies, once the candidates are elected into office, their social media efforts don't end there. Once all of the effort is made during the campaign to gather, communicate with, and engage followers, fans, and online supporters, the winning candidate should never simply close up shop and abandon social media altogether. The key is finding the right and smartest strategies so the candidate can continue campaigning even after the win. Not only does social media networking engage the audience of the elected official, but it can even pave the way for the next election.

Returning to where we began, Representative Amash was one of the first legislators to share his votes via Facebook, a practice he began soon after joining the Michigan House of Representatives in 2009. As he shared with *National Review Online,* "We were dealing with budgets, and I decided, 'Maybe people at home would be interested in knowing what's going on here, minute by minute ... I started posting things on the floor and how I voted on a few things and people loved it."[1]

Indeed, this type of constituency relationship-building brought not only a well-spring of positive public response, but this level of authenticity and exchange marked the beginning of Amash's candidacy for U.S. Congress.

How Local Politicians Use Social Media

Social media is bringing politics to more of the average Joe and Jane than ever before. Since social media use is part of the daily routine for a large amount of American voters, social media is a medium that is making more Americans aware of the politicians in their local districts, on a state level, and federally. Before social media swept the Internet world by storm, many Americans may have had a hard time recognizing a local representative or councilman even if they were face-to-face or toe-to-toe with them. Social media has changed the political literacy of most Americans, allowing them to not only recognize these politicians and representatives, but to also be more engaged on a personal level. The level of awareness of the average American has increased, which means that more educated voters are hitting the polls and Americans are becoming more engaged in the political realm that surrounds them locally and nationally.

The engagement that the social media platform provides is not going unnoticed either because more politicians are using the medium as a communication tool, even after the election is over. Primarily, elected candidates are using social media as a platform for creating conversations and interacting with the public.

Consider Massachusetts (D) Governor Deval Patrick, who employs Brad Blake as his director of new media and online strategy. This means that 100 percent of Blake's job is social media management. Blake oversees content from the Governor's office via Twitter, YouTube, and Flickr, updating the Governor's website, and even press releases that go out to the media. Governor Patrick's office started his Facebook page and Facebook fan page when the Governor was campaigning, but these continued to play an integral part when the Governor was elected into office. The Governor's office reports that social media interaction provides a platform where they are "constantly learning and listening to our users and those in both government and web 2.0 to tweak what we do and do it better."[2]

Blake mentions the use of social media played an integral role in pulling off an online community forum event. The online forum brought together representatives from 146 cities and towns in the state of Massachusetts. "To bring those people together to work in a public space without using social media would have been extremely difficult and resource-intensive. And we had very little media attention for that forum—it was mostly through social media that people found out about it. Not to turn it into a contest... but compared to President Obama's Open Government Brainstorm website that was launched one week earlier than ours and active for 15 more days, Governor Patrick's Forum had 29 percent more members per capita and 99 percent more comments per capita."[3]

Secretary of State for Kentucky, Republican Trey Grayson, who in January of 2011 resigned his position to become Director of Harvard's Institute of Politics, began using social media in 2006, the tip of the iceberg in a series of technology innovations designed to give citizens greater access to government. His online measures led to international awards for its outstanding government website. For example,

> The Office became the first agency in Kentucky to post its 'checkbook' online and become a model for transparency in the state. At the conclusion of the administration, over 7 million images, ranging from corporate documents to original land patents, are now available online. Historians have praised the Office for making full-color images of the state's original land patents available, making the Office a leader in this area nationally. Grayson also placed the Governor's Executive Journal online so that citizens had immediate access to actions their government was taking.[4]

The Tea Party Rides on Social Media

A group of Americans got together after the American Recovery and Reinvestment Act of 2009 and started the Tea Party movement. The Tea Party movement celebrated its first anniversary on February 27, 2010.

The group is unique in their utilization of Facebook, Twitter, MySpace and Blogs, as well as their extreme exposure on Fox News. Because they are a grass roots movement, most of their collaborating is done online and through viral marketing.

In April, 2009, they agreed to demonstrate on "Tax Day." Multitudes turned out across the county. The movement quickly became a sprawling rebellion with multiplying citizens attending rallies while sharing information online and mobilizing to support or oppose certain candidates.

Glenn Beck with Fox News stated that elite media is trying to prevent the Tea Party movement from receiving attention, but that Fox & Friends would support them in the strongest way.

Arnold Schwarzenegger criticized the Tea Party movement as something that will "twinkle and disappear." On the contrary, it is spreading to the United Kingdom where many are creating events to gather and vent, mostly through individual blogs.

Word spread as people gathered in churches and groups started tweeting about the movement. One major Tea Party website is http://www.teapartypatriots.org/Default.aspx. When logging into this site, there are two important options—the option to blog, as well as tweet on behalf of the cause.

As of spring 2010, Tea Party movement followers on Facebook had over 96,000 fans; Twitter—1,200 followers and YouTube—204 subscribers. Tea Partiers obviously followed Obama's campaign strategy.

The new media age enables users to collaborate and interact. One person sends out a thread to a "not so interested" group, but they still skim over it. One of those people decides to broadcast that information, creating a domino effect.

Social media is wildly inexpensive relative to traditional media outlets; it is generally unedited, and more people pay attention to it because users tend to feel personally closer to the fellow community members.

HOW IS THE TEA PARTY MOVEMENT USING THE INTERNET AGE, I.E. TWITTER, TO IT'S ADVANTAGE? Topics in Digital Media—spring '10.Name of author not given.
"<http://cultureandcommunication.org/tdm/s10/03/01/tea-party/. >"
"<http://www.silive.com/opinion/columns/index.ssf/2010/07/tea_party_a_legitimate_grassro.html, >"
"<http://www.teapartypatriots.org/Default.aspx.>"

These changes were not the result of massive budget increases. In fact, as noted in an office press release, "All of these accomplishments come in spite of deep budget cuts to the Office. During the last full fiscal year of Grayson's administration, the Office operated from a budget 15% less than the one he inherited when he was sworn in."[5]

On the west coast, San Francisco Mayor Gavin Newsom too has engaged social media as a tool to create conversations between government officials and the people the officials serve in office. Some of the ways that Mayor Newsom uses social media includes his DataSF campaign. This campaign provides citizens with access to city data such as housing, health, transportation, and public safety. The program is described as "open data site, which provides "structured, raw and machine-readable government data to the public in an easily downloadable format"[6] all of which is designed to offer access and transparency.

In Brownsville, Texas, Melissa Zamora, City Commissioner of District 3, uses social media as a means of increasing the amount of engagement she has with her constituents. Zamora finds that her constituents are more willing and able to voice their opinions using social media networks and outlets because it is a fast and easy way for them to become involved. Since constituents are able to "voice support or opposition through a few keystrokes, there is more feedback."[7]

Not only are politicians using social media as a platform for creating conversations, but social media also plays an integral role in creating change.

In Elgin, Illinois, Cristina Castro, the Commissioner of Kane County Board 20th District, employs Facebook and Twitter to collect feedback from her constituents. She also uses social media tools to share news articles, alert followers of upcoming meetings, and to elicit feedback on time-sensitive or pending issues in the community. She finds social media as a tool that provides direct access to her constituents and vice versa. Castro notes that "government needs to be transparent and by utilizing social media, it allows me to actively provide them with information they need in a timely and real-time fashion."[8]

Social Media is Part of the Strategy

It is important that politicians and their staff understand that social media is one of the many tools they can use to engage, communicate with, and elicit feedback from constituents. In other words, social media is one piece of the overall communication strategy. For example, Blake customizes which social media tools he uses for the Governor based on the situation at hand. He shares, "What I try to do, both internally and when working with others on using social media is to talk about the need or communication gap first, then figure out which tools best fill that need or gap."[9]

Heading up to the northeast, New York State Assemblyman Micah Kellner also uses multiple social media outlets and platforms to engage constituents in the 65th Assembly District. For him, Facebook and his blog have proven to be the most effective communication platforms, but he also goes on to say that "all of these tools work best when they're integrated—when we use each of them in a way that's complementary to the others. Rather than focus on them primarily as separate pieces, I prefer to think of them as parts of our overall communications strategy."[10]

While individual elected officials have been employing social media as part of their communication tools, political groups in general are also reaping the benefits of these communication platforms. For example, activist groups have been using social media platforms as a way to educate voters on elected officials, such as the ways constituents can contact these representatives either online or offline. According to a strategist for the web technology forum Advomatic Julie Blitzer, "These tools are just one more mechanism to direct activists to traditional elected official contact methods: writing letters and calling."[11]

Co-founder of ProjectVirginia, designed to help Republican candidates utilize social media and web technology, Steve Pearson notes that social media is one tool that is imperative for modern political campaigns and modern means for politicians in office to communicate with voters and constituents. Person's firm helps to educate political candidates and elected officials on how to use social media tools such as Facebook, YouTube, Digg and Twitter to disseminate political messages and engage their audiences.

Pearson says, "You can't give the same stump speech. You have to come up with new stuff every day...That's the fundamental challenge of the new medium."[12]

The Human Side of Social Media in Politics

Without the individual constituents social media could never be as powerful a tool as it is for politicians in office. First, it is the burning desire and need that humans have to gather political information. Second, it is the need and the want to share their own perspectives with the politicians they have elected into office (or are representing them even if they did not elect them in the first place). Social interaction is a key element to human nature and social media provides the platform for individuals to find this social interaction, even on a political level, and even when it is not in a face-to-face situation. According to Secretary Grayson, "They have the opportunity to see that I am not just some figurehead sitting behind a desk at the Capitol. They get to see the personal me and understand why I make certain decisions."[13]

Assemblyman Kellner agrees saying that "Politics is about conversation, and personal, face-to-face interaction is still the foundation of that, especially at the local level." This belief leads Kellner to use social media as a platform that allows for "broadening my overall efforts to engage with the community I represent."[14]

While 2008 may be the year that officially launched the use of modern technology such as social media as a platform for campaigning and continuing the conversations with constituents once in office, social media is quickly emerging as the dividing line between those elected officials in office who succeed and those not using social media who have not harnessed the power of this highly effective communication tool.

Once an election is over, use of social media becomes even more important for an elected official because it's a means of proving out the vote and building immediate support to a reelection campaign. While all of the usual-suspect social media platforms should be deployed, it behooves any elected official to take stock in his or her government's web pages first and foremost.

If an official is busy tweeting from an elected perch, but the average citizen can't purchase a license for a pet, or voice a concern about a new regulation, than the official has missed the boat on providing relevance and value to those being served. Attention to social media networks before a candidate needs them, gives that individual a definite advantage entering the next election because people will already have had the opportunity to form a relationship with and gain an understanding of who the candidate is, along with how that candidate is able to lead.

Tips for Using Social Media in Office

If you ask Twitter and Facebook followers what they are looking for when politicians use social media, you are likely to hear descriptive words such as "be yourself, real, and interact instead of broadcasting."[15]

Be a Real Person. When possible, elected officials should really be using the social media tools rather than have a dedicated staff member doing it for them. Nobody can be as real as the official and when the elected official conducts his or her own social media conversations and interactions, it is more real and genuine. Think of it as inviting your constituents to have a cup of coffee with you. Be yourself, let your personality shine through, and share yourself and information that your coffee buddy can relate to, understand, and appreciate.

Interaction is the Key. Using social media while in office is not simply about throwing up a profile on the social media networks. On the contrary, interacting with your friends, fans, and followers is the key to interacting with the people who put you in the office in the first place. When someone makes a comment or poses a question to you on your social media platforms, respond. Using social media as a communication tool has the same rules as when someone emails you or sends a letter to your office; you have to answer them.

You can also interact in the other direction by monitoring conversations that are taking place about issues that are of interest to you. Monitor online newspapers and websites that are writing about these issues and leave your own comments or pose your own questions.

Mind Your Social Manners. Never forget that what you post on your online platforms remain there forever, even if you delete them. This means you need to be very aware and hypersensitive to what you say and how you say it. Approach writing your updates and your interactions as the professional that you are, so that nothing comes back to tarnish your reputation or platform later.

Be Diverse. Social media use is not only about typing up an update on your thoughts on an issue or which meeting you are currently attending. Social media is multi-media, which means you can use other mediums of communication such as pictures, videos, and audio files. Not only should you be using a variety of media to get your message across, but you should also be using these mediums on various platforms such as your blog, YouTube, iTunes,

Flickr, Facebook, Twitter, your website, and the list simply goes on and on.

Follow the Big Dogs. If you are still not sure how you can use social media while in office or are looking for new ways to use social media, then follow what the big dogs are doing on these networks. By no means does this require you or suggest that you copy what someone else is doing but you can certainly draw inspiration. Follow political candidates, other elected officials, and even social media experts to gather ideas that you can implement as part of your own social media strategy while in office.

Even World Leaders Use Social Media. You saw the power of social media during the Obama campaign and you continue to see how powerful a tool it can be while he is in office as the leader of this country. By no means, however, is Obama alone in using social media as part of the overall communication plan for elected officials. At least four other leaders emerge as examples of how to use social media to communicate and connect with interested parties.

If you still have doubts on how powerful a tool social media can be in politics, consider that at the time of this writing, Barack Obama had more than 9 million followers on Twitter and more than 22 million on Facebook; Hugo Chavez had close to 1.8 million followers on Twitter and close to 151,000 Facebook fans; and Sarah Palin had 600,000 Twitter followers and more than 3 million Facebook fans.

While more and more political campaigns are employing social media as a major communication tool in getting officials into office and fundraising throughout the campaign process, even more elected officials are coming to understand how to continue to harness the power of social media after the win. It makes sense to continue the effort made during the campaign to gather, communicate with, and engage followers, fans, and online supporters, rather than close up shop and abandon social media altogether. The key is finding the right social media strategies so the candidate can continue campaigning even after the win to engage the audience and even pave the way for the next election—and the next win.

1 Boulduc, B. (2010, September 2). "Facebook the Nation." *National Review Online.* http://www. nationalreview.com/articles/245403/face book-nation-brian-bolduc#

2 Sternberg, J. (2009, October 19). How Local Politicians Are Using Social Media. *Mashable.* http:// mashable.com/2009/10/19/social-media-local-politics/

3 Sternberg, J.

4 McAdam, T. (2011, January 31). "Kentucky's Secretary of State, Trey Grayson, Resigns, Goes to Harvard." *Louisville City Hall Examiner.* http://www.examiner.com/city-hall-in-louisville/ kentucky-s-secretary-of-state-trey-grayson-resigns-goes-to-harvard

5 Grayson Ends Tenure, Leaving Legacy of Efficiency, Productivity, and Civility. (2011, January 28). http://sos.ky.gov/NR/exeres/07B8FF41-2A3E-4BBB-8740-87F30E8CE74A.htm

6 Fretwell, L. (2009, December 21). San Francisco's DataSF Launch. http://govfresh.com/2009/12/san-francisco-announces-launch-of-datasf-org/

7 Moving Toward a 21st Century Right-To-Know Agenda. (2008, November 14). http://issuu.com/ ombwatch/docs/21strtkrecs

8 Sternberg, J.

9 Lyon, E. (2010, June 17). Using Social Media to Rally Support for Politicians. http://sparxoo. com/2010/06/17/using-social-media-to-rally-support-for-politicians/

10 Sternberg, J.

11 Sternberg, J.

12 Creamer, M. (2010, November 1). Social media connects campaigns, voters. *Lodi News-Sentinel.* http://www.lodinews.com/news/article_a7b8297f-d60d-50cc-b525-3885d7d9a940.html

13 Sevasti, A. (2010, October 13). Five World Leaders Using Social Media Effectively. *Memeburn.* http://memeburn.com/2010/10/five-world-leaders-using-social- media-effectively/

14 Sevasti, A.

15 Doland, G. (2009, August 14). Tips for Politicians Using Social Media. *The New Mexico Independent.* http://newmexicoindependent.com/33986/tips-for-politicians-using-social-media

AFTERWORD

Your Next Campaign Starts Before the Polls Close

ONCE A CANDIDATE has been elected, the tendency had been to close up campaign headquarters and end the chapter called campaigning. The time-shifted, ever-present, online campaign stop means never really closing one's campaign in the sense that once a candidate has gotten a voter's attention, it would be a shame to stop the conversation midstream. Thus, we are seeing the shift to "campaign-lite" in non-campaign periods, where elected officials are able to maintain a steady, updated, online presence and conversation with their constituents, both as a means of moving them from voting them into office, to sustained support through advocacy on policy issues.

Activities such as updating profiles, posting press releases, voting decisions, policy positions, and more can help to keep a candidate in the public eye during the time in which he or she is holding office. This can help a candidate to guard against having to reintroduce him or herself to voters when the election cycle comes around again. But keep in mind that being in a constant state of campaigning can do an elected official more harm than good. Bear in mind that once a candidate is elected, it is time to start serving, and making the case for why you were a good choice based on actions instead of ongoing promises. Offering updates, signs of progress, and value-adds does the job of continuing the conversation in an authentic, genuine way.

Building Long-Term Relationships

Most elected officials don't get into politics to run once and retire from office. They aim to win successively and to make a career of serving the interests of the public. Thus, the focus must always be on building a solid reputation, staying out in front of the voters, and shaping the desired image for today, next year, and next election.

Shaping a public track record can give an elected official a distinct advantage against an opponent who might be a newcomer with no known background of voting decisions or proven leadership. Ongoing networking efforts can help to garner future volunteers, as well as shape positioning based on ongoing insights from the public. Continued efforts can also help to let the voter base know that you appreciate their continued support. Beyond posting a "thank you" on your webpage after a win, your online networks can be used to share progress reports, opportunities for constituents to engage, and more.

In addition to content generation, you will also want to become an ardent content consumer. You may wish to consider opening a Google Reader Account and searching those sites that are directly discussing topics or issues that pertain to your sphere of influence. Your goal is to become well versed on every trend that is or will be affecting your messaging and your upcoming campaign. Post any relevant issues to your blog or Twitter feed and encourage discussion. This will go a long way toward building your reputation as an engaged official.

When we consider the rich arsenal of tools at our disposal for engaging, cultivating, soliciting, and stewarding those who voted for your candidate, and supported him or her financially and through grassroots efforts, it is clear that social media offers the perfect model for what campaigns strive to do: start a conversation with their base of support and then continue that conversation not only through election night, but through the term of office, to the next election cycle, and ultimately, through a lifetime of engaged support.

Social media success rises and falls based on this ongoing engagement, making these online channels the ideal vehicles for achieving long-term relationship building. We must keep in mind that while we must avoid taking the "next shiny object" approach to the channels we create, we must pay close attention to how our base of support continues to evolve, be it in terms of the social networking platforms they are using more (or less), or the technologies they are most closely aligned with (e.g., mobile devices, laptops, iPods or iPads, e-readers, and more).

The most important piece of advice for anyone working within a political campaign is that we must avoid shaping our communications strategies solely on platforms or networks that we do not control, but rather, we must focus on the value-added content, itself, so that when we find our audiences moving from Twitter to Twitter-plus, or from Friendster to the next iteration of a Facebook network, we will be prepared to move seamlessly and nimbly with an eye toward sustaining the engagement while remaining top of mind as the candidate of choice in a sea of worthy causes.

We must compete not only on the core of our missions, but also on our abilities to travel and grow with our core of supporters, while considering the needs of the next generation of supporters. Most of what we do within the context of politics is about connecting in the short-term for a long-term, multi-generational effect.

Social media provides the ideal mix of tools for accomplishing beyond the must-do's and driving us into engagements we may once have considered beyond our reach. This enables us to break free of the almost universal concerns from supporters such as, "You only contact us when you want our money or out vote," or "Every time I turn around, Campaign X is asking me for something else." Volunteer and donor fatigue are real and growing concerns for any political campaign, hence social media accomplishes the task of opening up new and ongoing opportunities for support from new pipelines of individuals who might be willing to engage.

We are in the midst of an exciting sea change in the ways in which we build relationships with core constituencies, and while we haven't yet landed, we have amassed sufficient data to know that (a) even as it continues to evolve, social media is here to stay; (b) while voter interest will continue to ebb and flow based on perceived skin in the game by the average citizen, never before have political campaigns had such unbridled access to existing and new target groups; and (c) sitting on the sidelines of social media is no longer acceptable for any campaign, in that you risk becoming invisible at best, and at worst, irrelevant.

Any candidate who is serious about running must use the content presented here as a launching pad for beginning or growing a social media strategy. Remember that this strategy must be incorporated into broader marketing and communications efforts (e.g., door-to-door stops, direct mail, phon-a-thons), and the campaign must always maintain an iterative approach through listening to constituents and then pouring this knowledge back into the next campaign speech, event, or appeal.

For those who feel they have missed the social-media train, there is always another train, and starting now means taking advantage of the best practices that have been shaped by colleagues and competitors. No campaign can afford to take a pass, and each entity will bring its own level of creativity and understanding to the process of shaping a sound social media plan for the purpose of shaping a winning campaign.

It is in this spirit that I wish you the very best of luck in your efforts to advance your campaign goals and your candidate's aspirations through some of the most dynamic and powerful relationship-building strategies the political arena has ever seen. As has been the case with the close of each of the books in the *Survival Guide* series, I encourage you to share your experiences with me. You can do so by sending an email to contact@socialmediasurvivalguide.com. I would love to hear from you, and welcome the opportunity to help share your story with others in an upcoming publication.

BONUS ONLINE EXTRAS

Download two great tools for campaign success:

Are You Ready to Run for Office?: Take the Readiness Test to Determine If You're Ready to Announce Your Campaign

Candidate Checklist: Top 10 Social Media Must-Haves for Winning Elections

**Visit
www.SocialMediaSurvivalGuideForPoliticalCampaigns.com**

The Social Media Survival Guide Series

Just as organizations and individuals are eager to embrace the opportunity, they are hesitant to take on additional risk, leaving many to fall behind the competition in the wake of uncertainty. **The Social Media Survival Guide** and its companion titles are designed to make social media accessible, tactical and easy to use right away. **The Survival Guide** series will help you to market successfully within this space, maintain a competitive edge and boost results—from increasing sales, to landing the job, to winning elections.

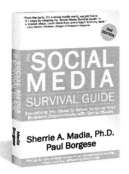

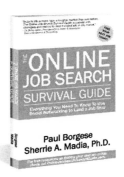
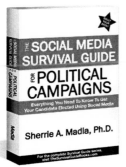
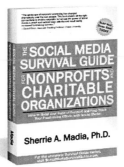

The Social Media Survival Guide:
Everything You Need to Know to Grow Your Business Exponentially with Social Media

The Social Media Survival Guide (Spanish-language edition)

The Online Job Search Survival Guide:
Everything You Need to Know to Use Social Networking to Land a Job Now

The Social Media Survival Guide for Political Campaigns:
Everything You Need to Know to Get Your Candidate Elected Using Social Media

The Social Media Survival Guide for Nonprofit and Charitable Organizations: How to Build
Your Base of Support and Fast-Track Your Fundraising Efforts with Social Media

Order at SocialMediaSurvivalGuide.com

CPSIA information can be obtained at www.ICGtesting.com
Printed in the USA
LVOW091004271111

256604LV00012B/47/P